# REVISION

BY

*KIT REED*

CINCINNATI, OHIO

# ABOUT THE AUTHOR

Kit Reed is a novelist who teaches student writers at Wesleyan University in Connecticut. Her short stories have appeared in magazines ranging from *Cosmopolitan* and *Missouri Review* to *The Magazine of Fantasy and Science Fiction*. In addition to her eleven novels and four short story collections, she has published *Story First: The Writer as Insider*, a widely used text for writers of fiction. Her most recent novel, *Catholic Girls*, is now in paperback. A member of the National Book Critics Circle, Kit Reed is a frequent reviewer of fiction for publications, including *The New York Times Book Review*.

**Revision.** Copyright ©1989 by Kit Reed. Printed and bound in the United States of America. All rights reserved. No part of this book may be reproduced in any form or by any electronic or mechanical means including information storage and retrieval systems without permission in writing from the publisher, except by a reviewer, who may quote brief passages in a review. Published by Writer's Digest Books, an imprint of F&W Publications, 1507 Dana Ave., Cincinnati, Ohio 45207. First edition.

93 92 91 90 89     5 4 3 2 1

Library of Congress Cataloging-in-Publication Data

Reed, Kit.
  Revision/by Kit Reed
  p.   cm.
  Includes index.
ISBN 0-89879-350-5
  1. Authorship.   I. Title.
PN145.R35   1989                    88-31296
                                       CIP

*for Lois Gould*

# Also by Kit Reed

**Novels:**
*Mother Isn't Dead She's Only Sleeping*
*At War as Children*
*The Better Part*
*Cry of the Daughter*
*Armed Camps*
*Tiger Rag*
*Captain Grownup*
*The Ballad of T. Rantula*
*Magic Time*
*Fort Privilege*
*Catholic Girls*

**Short Story Collections:**
*Mr. Da V. and Other Stories*
*The Killer Mice*
*Other Stories and: The Attack of the Giant Baby*
*The Revenge of the Senior Citizens * Plus*

**Texts:**
*Story First: The Writer as Insider*
*Revision*

# CONTENTS

# Preface

If you could buy a document or a piece of magic that would enable you to write successful fiction, if you could learn one thing that would make you able to write successful stories and novels, how much would you be willing to pay? Ten dollars? A hundred? A thousand?

How far would you be willing to go to get it?

Most of us who make a life in fiction would spend every penny we have and call it cheap at the price. We would travel to Katmandu or China to find the key.

Now for the trick question.

What if the secret to success in this case turned out to be not a matter of parting with dollars and cents, but of expenditure of time? How many hours would you be willing to spend? Ten? A hundred? A thousand?

If most of us would happily spend thousands for the secret to success, then it makes sense for us to spend as many hours as it takes to find it.

Surprisingly, many writers—particularly beginning writers—are skinflints here.

They're ready to give everything but the time.

Many of us get so committed to what we already have on the page that we will do anything to avoid rewriting. Yet it's the extra time that makes the difference.

Fledgling writers are often so excited by what they are doing that they never get past the first draft. There's nothing like that first flush of accomplishment. Look what I did! The sense of pleasure and wonder often outstrips what's on the page. So do expectations. Many beginners think a piece of work is wonderful not because of what it is, but because they wrote it. One adult class I taught at Wesleyan University turned in their first exercises convinced they were going to sell them to the magazines immediately and thus recoup the cost of tuition.

Their first lesson turned out to be a hard one: *everything you write is not perfect.*

The second was easier: *But you can make it better.* How? Through revision.

An important first step, then, is *keeping an open mind.* This means being willing to reconsider. Many student writers would rather argue than think through something they have written, going to any lengths to defend rather than rewrite what's already on the page. The best ones understand that no matter how hard they've worked or how pleased they are, what they have is probably only a beginning. Some discover that they're draft writers. That "story" they handed in turns out to be not a story but rather raw material which they will cut, shape, expand and reorganize over several weeks until it becomes a finished story. Others, who revise as they go, word for word, sentence for sentence, page for page, learn that even though the work may be polished, it isn't finished. It may need cutting here, expansion there — the kind of dramatic development that makes it more accessible to the reader.

Writing "The End" does not necessarily mean you are finished. It means you are finished with *this draft.* For the time being. Until it becomes clear what you need to do next.

Nobody enjoys this moment of truth. Professionals who have given their all to a story or a novel only to run into editorial criticism feel most of the same things beginning writers do: commitment to the vision that made them begin the work in the first place, distress at the idea that *after all that work* it's still not ready.

We don't necessarily expect praise when we turn in a piece of work we are proud of, but we are brought up short by anything less than acceptance. Remember, professionals revise as part of the process of composition. We've already spent tens or hundreds or thousands of hours writing and rewriting to create what we think is the final version.

Then our first reader doesn't get it. Or our agent or an editor doesn't get it. Or one or the other thinks it's going to be good as soon as we make revisions.

Our first instinct may be to argue. Some of us go through all the classic stages—rage, denial, depression, bargaining and acceptance. In the end we're going to listen to editorial comments, dig in and rewrite. Again. Again. Revising, we close the distance between the work at hand and publication. Until it's published, we can't hope to reach more than a handful of readers.

If we cared enough to write the work in the first place, we certainly care enough about it to rewrite it.

We know it's the only way to reach our audience.

Working writers know that there are no tricks, no special documents that automatically entitle a writer to success, but there is a way. This book is designed to help you find it.

It is revision.

It takes guts, persistence and a heart of steel for beginning writers to turn revision into an organic part of their working equipment, but it can be done, and once you begin, you're going to see immediate payoffs. Those of us who have been around for a while can tell you that revision is far easier than inventing something in the first place. It goes faster and it makes your work better.

Forget about money for the time being.

Be willing to spend the time.

## CHAPTER 1

# NOTHING YOU WRITE IS CARVED IN STONE

I'M TOLD THAT NOT EVERYBODY out there resists the idea of revision—that there are, in fact, beginning writers who plunge in joyfully without having to be encouraged. Those of you who are already happily engaged in revision as a way of life are encouraged to move on to the later chapters—Chapter Three and everything that follows.

I do, however, want to point out that I've learned through working with undergraduate writers that a great many beginning writers *think* they're revising when they've made a few superficial changes. Even attitudes sometimes need revision.

As for those of you who revise endlessly as a way of putting off the inevitable moment of judgment—or, in fact, beginning something new—I have words for you, which will come in Chapter Twelve: Knowing When to Quit.

In the meantime I'm going to assume that many of you have picked up this book precisely because you know there's something you ought to be doing but you need encouragement because you can't quite bring yourself to do it. For you, I offer a cautionary tale, in hopes that I can help you shortcut a few hard lessons.

## ONE WRITER'S STORY

Like you, I was interested in audience—I wanted one. Unfortunately, I used to think everything I wrote was wonderful even

4

before I finished it. Like so many beginning writers I was hung up on the amateur's concept of inspiration. I transferred the voices I heard directly to the page—too fast. The fact that the words came so easily convinced me they must be right—whether or not they were. I thought each story was wonderful just because I wrote it.

Since then, I've made a number of painful discoveries, which I've organized here in hopes they may help you.

## Rule One: Your First Thoughts Are Not Necessarily Your Best Thoughts.

I remember thinking if readers didn't get what I was trying to do the first time I wrote a story, it was because they were stupid, not because there might be a problem with the story. In spite of negative signals from the outside world—teachers' comments on my papers, and later, printed rejection slips in droves—I believed in myself as a writer. In order to believe in myself as a writer, I thought, I had to believe in everything I wrote. I wrote it, which meant it must be right . . .—Didn't it?

It took me three years of hard work and heavy losses to learn that getting it right involved more than just getting it written.

## Rule Two: Nothing You Write Is Carved in Stone.

Well, who knew? Encouraged by an easy first sale, I had decided that not only could I write, I could be a good writer without much effort. By the time I learned that I wasn't good every time, and I wasn't necessarily good on a first draft, I had written some twenty-two stories a year for three years and not sold any of them. I had a hit-or-miss attitude toward what I was doing, thinking that if I fired enough rounds of buckshot out into the world, sooner or later I was going to hit my market.

I see now that it would have made more sense for me to spend all the time it took to perfect a single guided missile designed to hit its target the first time out.

But I was only a beginner, hung up on pride. In spite of the kindness of an agent who read and said she could not sell any of these stories, I pinned her responses on bad judgment. If she said a story wasn't right for the marketplace, I thought it must be because I was committing *art* while she was, after all, in business. Unfortunately, I wasn't enough of a grownup about my writing to learn by revising. Getting a story back from my disappointed reader at the agency, I never reread it and I certainly never rewrote it. Instead I would write another and fire it off.

Perhaps because we need it to survive in a world which is not necessarily crying out for our stories, most writers of fiction are born with a protective sense of self-confidence. We have to believe in ourselves before anybody else will. Unfortunately, there is a thin line between healthy self-confidence and blind vanity, and it's all too easy for us to slip across it.

Even when these early stories I wrote boomeranged, coming back almost by return mail, I was too blind—and deaf to criticism—to get the message.

In a way, you could say that during this miserable period I was teaching myself to write, but there were problems. Of the stories I wrote in those three years not one was published. I have little memory of them. Not even the manuscripts survive, which is probably just as well, given my slapdash attitude. If I still had them I'd be embarrassed to look at them—the flashes of talent, thin ideas, the serious problems with narrative.

All those hours of work! All those wasted words! All that blasted hope!

What if I had paid the two dollars, driven the five miles, gone the rest of the way around the block?

At the time, I couldn't bring myself to do it.

I remember thinking that if I didn't get a story right the first time, I didn't want to spend any more time on it. This accounts for all the abandoned efforts, mailed out three or four times to magazines, returned rejected, and after a brief period of mourning, put away forever.

I remember thinking I'd rather scrub floors or write a whole new story than rewrite an old one. Remember, I was a beginning writer.

As a writer who's survived, I hope you'll learn from my mistakes—and my all-too-gradual discovery that revision is a part of every successful writer's working equipment.

## Rule Three: It Takes Revision to Turn a Loss into a Win.

At the time, pride stood between me and what I wanted. I needed to go the rest of the distance to become a professional. It was a hard lesson for an undisciplined beginning writer.

It took years for me to learn how to step outside the work—how to distance myself so I could see clearly exactly what I was doing. We'll talk about this at length in Chapter Four: How to Find Out Whether You're Finished When You Think You're Finished.

## Rule Four: Shortstop Criticism—Be Your Own Toughest Critic.

Sometimes even before I'd mailed a story, I suspected there might be a problem with it. But with the false optimism of certain medical patients, I mailed it anyway, in hopes nobody would notice. It was like going to the doctor and failing to mention a specific symptom: if the doctor doesn't notice this symptom that's bothering me, then my problem is not serious.

I mailed my flawed stories thinking, If they don't notice there is a problem, then there's nothing the matter with these stories.

Who did I think *they* were? Who did I think I was, imagining I might be able to fool them?

*They* turned out to be the audience these stories never reached, the audience I would not reach until I learned to identify problems with each piece of work and solve them by rewriting.

In baseball, the shortstop catches the ball before it reaches the outfield or goes over the fence and loses the game for you. As I learned—on the job, and over a period of years—revision fulfills some of the same functions. It helps writers catch story flaws before they lose the reader.

## *Rule Five: If It's Worth Doing at All, It's Worth Doing Right.*

Some writers are lucky enough to learn this on the job at the very beginning. Their early work is good enough to attract the attention of an editor who may want to publish it if they are willing to do the necessary revision. Such writers begin getting short notes at the bottom of those printed rejection slips from magazines, suggestions for revision that may lead to a sale. A publisher is interested in doing a novel—if the writer is willing to develop and perfect this scene, answer those questions, cut this section or expand that.

Others develop a healthy respect for revision in graduate writing programs all over the country, where battle-scarred professionals teach by example, or they may learn in the give-and-take of workshops in which fellow students criticize from the craftsman's point of view. Looking at student work in several drafts, they talk in detail about how to close the distance between what the student has in mind and what is on the page.

The rest of us have to learn on our own, working alone, with nobody to let us know how we're doing except those disembodied editors who keep sending rejection slips.

I'd like to say that for me the light dawned all at once, that I was converted overnight from careless pride to careful craftsmanship, but it seems I was a slow learner.

In time I figured out that if I had written sixty-six stories in three years and failed to place *even one of them*, maybe this was not the fault of doltish readers or the result of cruel fate.

It was not their problem.

It was my problem.

There just might be something the matter with the work.

Knowing there is a problem and doing something about it are two different things. I was fortunate enough to be belted along by three things: 1. editorial feedback in the form of one splendid reader at home and a market-minded reader in a literary agency, 2. increasingly lengthy editorial notes on rejection slips and 3. habits learned in the newsrooms of two city newspapers.

It's clear that sooner or later I was going to figure out that I had to start rewriting my fiction in order to make it do what I wanted. Techniques learned in the newsroom helped me go about it. I will talk about this at length in Chapter Three: Kinds of Revision.

What fascinates me now, looking back, is the fact that it never crossed my mind to object to revising in the newsroom. It was part of my job. Since I already thought of myself as a novelist-in-hiding, I was clearly less protective of my nonfiction. It seemed more important to get it into acceptable form to go into the paper than to stand around defending what I had already written.

A competent craftsman, I wrote and rewrote cheerfully, preparing news and feature stories for city editors in Florida and Connecticut. Because I had to recast the news lead—the opening of each story—as many times as it took me to get everything in and get it *right*, I got used to proceeding in exactly the same way every time I sat down to write. I composed and rewrote sentence by sentence, cutting where necessary to come up with a tight and well-organized story, to forestall complaints from city desk and questions from the copy editors. I was shortstopping criticism—in the newsroom, at least.

If the desk wasn't satisfied, I had to rewrite.

As a reporter I grew more and more careful about perfecting what I turned in because in the best of all possible worlds I would be corrected, or yelled at; in the worst, there was the outside possibility that I might get fired. Instead I ended up winning prizes for reporting.

Yet when I quit and began writing fiction full time, it was as if I had learned nothing. I can't now explain why I imagined writing fiction would be any different, but I did. It was, after all, fiction. Maybe I thought writing news and committing *art* were not the same things, but I can't for the life of me understand why I thought that unlike news writing, fiction could sprout in an untended garden.

After five years in a newsroom, I may have felt somehow released. Maybe I had the illusion that since this was fiction I could do anything I wanted and expect it to work out right the first time. After all, I thought, wasn't I inspired?

But there were those sixty-six unpublishable short stories.

It was only when I began applying newsroom techniques to fiction—typing and retyping sentence by sentence, paragraph by paragraph, page by page until I got something *right*—that my fiction turned into anything better than the hasty efforts of a gifted amateur.

Digging my feet in, moving reluctantly, I found my way into revision. I can't pinpoint the moment at which I began that first revision, but I remember what I felt:

1. Oh wow, this isn't so bad.
2. Hey, *this story is getting better*.

And I remember what happened. *I began selling more stories.*

Learning hard, I learned well. I can't think of any other way to write.

## Rule Six: Extra Effort Closes the Distance between You and Your Audience.

In my time I have done up to five revisions of a novel I thought was finished before it left my hands on its first submission; I do so many sentence and page drafts that I counted seventeen attempts at the first page of my sixth novel, and those were only the ones I could manage to round up for a text on writing, *Story First: The Writer as Insider*. They went into an appendix titled, *Once More Through the Typewriter*.

The title bears some discussion. A Pulitzer Prizewinning friend who wishes to remain nameless at one point showed my resident critic and me a draft of a novel which, as it turned out, was not published until ten years later, at which time it earned him a quarter of a million dollars.

Both of us felt this early draft by a prizewinning author was not quite right but my resident critic found precisely the way to say it: "I think this ought to go once more through the typewriter."

An established professional, our friend took this in precisely the way it was intended. He put his new novel through the type-writer not once more but seven times. The seventh draft reached an enormous audience in hardcover, through book clubs and in paperback.

Then there's my eleventh novel. Remember this is a novel I wrote in sentence and page drafts in the first version, shaping, discarding, trying my best *at every stage* to make it as good as I could make it. The working papers for the first draft fill a sizable carton. Attacking a second draft, I entered the novel into my computer. I'll talk more about this later. I have gangs of these cartons in the attic, representing all the false starts and developmental stages of what is turning out to be a long career in fiction.

As time passed, it became clear that there was still more work to do if I expected my novel ever to be published.

I felt all the usual things—pride, anger that others didn't see what I saw in the work, reluctance to work on it one more time after I thought it was finished—but I move through these stages faster now, and without histrionics.

If there was more work to do then I was going to have to do it, and for a compelling reason.

*I had to revise to reach my audience.*

If I cared enough to spend an enormous chunk of psychic energy and four-plus years on this particular novel in the first place, I certainly cared enough to put in the time and effort necessary to take it the rest of the way—in this case to publication, good reviews and paperback auction. It's clear to me that it's worth whatever it takes to move a manuscript from my desk to the readers who give it life outside my office.

## Rule Seven: Revision Means Survival.

Remember those twenty-two stories a year I wrote for three years without ever once turning my hand to a revision?

It's as if they were written by a different person. It's also clear to me that the different person who launched those stories like faulty kites and watched them crash was still an amateur.

Yes I learned to write while I was turning out three years' worth of flawed stories with no changes, no looking back and no time for second thoughts, but those sixty-six stories are forgotten. I can't help but wonder what I could have made of them if I had been willing and able to make myself spend the time to take them the rest of the way to an audience.

What if I had reread them before I mailed them in the first place? Gone back and put them once more through the typewriter? Twice? Three times?

What if I had listened to criticism, instead of wasting energy on arguing?

Revision might have turned some of those early losses into wins for me. It's clear that revision has worked for me again and again in the years since. An editor says: we may want to go ahead and publish this if you're willing to talk about revisions.

I don't waste time arguing. In many cases editors see what I can't—what the piece of work looks like to an outsider.

Editors and publishers can do something else I can't do for myself, unless I want to spend my life supporting vanity presses. They can buy my work and get it published. They take it to an audience.

I've told my embarrassing but all too common story at length in hopes it will speed you toward revision. Try to make revision part of your natural working equipment—a tool of the trade as essential as the instrument or machine you write with.

At this stage you should also know that once you've broken the sound barrier—cut through the beginner's initial resistance to reconsider and rework a story—you'll be amazed by results.

No, you haven't wrecked your story.

You've made it better.

What's more, since you've written it once, you already know how it comes out, which means you've developed second sight. Within the framework of the piece you're revising, you've acquired *the ability to see the future*. You can go back to the beginning and make all the signs point in the right direction.

Now, let's look at your own attitudes toward revision. Try to answer these questions honestly.

1. Do you ever rewrite?
   a. If so, when and why?
   b. If not, why not? Be a strict judge here.
2. Do you ever reread a piece after you think it's ready for submission?
3. Do you ever reread after you get negative criticism?
4. If you do reread, are you pleased or do you have misgivings?
5. If you're pleased with your work, do you care if readers agree with you?
6. Do you try to see whether readers are going to be just as pleased as you are? or:
7. Do you think criticism means not that you have a problem with the story, but that there's something the matter with the reader?
8. Do you make too many assumptions about your reader? Do you ever think:
   a. Any smart reader is going to "get" this.
   b. Anybody who doesn't get it doesn't deserve to get it.
   c. If it isn't quite right, readers are never going to notice.
9. If you reread a "finished" work and have misgivings, do you:
   a. Rework the story?
   b. Send it out anyway?
10. Do you ever think, I'll make revisions only if an editor/ publisher promises to buy it.
11. If you think you already revise quite enough, thank you, do you really? Does revision for you mean more than:
    a. Making a clean copy of the story you just wrote?
    b. Making a few superficial word changes?
12. Have you ever:
    a. Made significant cuts in a "finished" story?
    b. Reworked entire sentences, paragraphs or pages to complete your thinking?
    c. Found it necessary to reorganize a story so that everything points in the right direction?
    d. Revised to make certain scenes more dramatic?
    e. Further developed sections to make your intentions clear to the reader?

Now look at your answers, especially to the last two questions. Even if you honestly think you already revise—and like it—you're going to learn something.

If you've stopped at occasional word changes or called making a clean copy "revision," you have more work to do. If you are anything less than wholehearted in your desire to reconsider and rewrite—and do your utmost to complete your thinking and reach your reader—then it's time to make some changes.

And keep in mind my cautionary tale. I've confessed for a reason. If I can save you a year, or even ten days, then maybe those three years of busted short stories I wrote will have earned their keep. I want to help you cut through some of the painful stages of denial that cost me so much wasted time and effort.

By being willing to spend the extra time before a story leaves your desk, you're going to save time in the long run—the time it takes to reach an audience.

## CHAPTER 2

# HOW REVISION WORKS FOR YOU

I JUST GOT OFF THE PHONE with one of the denizens of the downtown Writers' Room, a place where New Yorkers who are professional writers rent space and move in with typewriters, computers or copy pencils. They like the Writers' Room because they work better in an office situation than they do at home. These include well-known novelists, biographers and writers of other nonfiction.

I called to ask my friend for a manuscript page to demonstrate how one established novelist goes about revision. She offered an early draft and finished page from her new novel, and her interest in the project sparked an exhibition about revision at the Writers' Room. Examples of rough drafts and finished pages filled the hall and drew national attention. You'll find them included in this book in the Appendix.

Everybody in the Writers' Room had something to contribute, because among professionals, everybody revises as part of the process. Except perhaps for Harlan Ellison, who says he completes revision in his head before he ever sits down at the typewriter, most established writers see their work through more than one version.

Without spelling out all the reasons we revise, most of us know we have to do it. It's part of our life. Although we may not be able to identify results before we reach the end of the road, we know there is a payoff. Revising, we are learning what we have to say while we figure out the best possible way to say it.

Some start by writing by hand and at a certain point convert to typewriter or computer. Others type or print a draft and then make pen or pencil changes between drafts, and still others make multiple changes as they go along, perfecting each sentence before they move on to the next one. We understand that we get even more from revision than we put into it. Sometimes, we're revising for immediate publication. At other times, with no immediate or specific market in prospect, we revise with even greater intensity because it helps us clarify and focus what we are doing.

In the case of some writers, a faithful exhibition of all the stages of even one paragraph revision would take up several display cases. No two first and last drafts look the same because no two writers work in exactly the same way, but one thing remains constant: everybody revises. A look at a couple of manuscripts will give you an idea what's going on.

We'll begin with a piece of student work because the gap or distance between first and later drafts is usually more pro-nounced in works by beginning writers. The immediate and obvious payoff makes revision particularly rewarding. Problems are more apparent and results are easier to see. Here is a passage from a student short story, reprinted with the author's permission.

I've duplicated his first version as it looked after I had read and put notes on it. Although they protest that they have rewritten their work before they turn it in, most undergraduate beginners are talking about one or two minor word changes. When we get together they admit this more or less cheerfully and, if we're going to work well together, they move on into more serious consideration of revision. Usually they're astounded by the results. Willingness to revise is perhaps the most important thing I have to teach them.

If my notes seem harsh here, remember, I am trying to do two things: to find out what this writer has to say and help him to say it better, and to get him used to bringing his work up to standard *before* it ever leaves his hands, even in the classroom.

The student and I talked through my notes on this passage, after which he sat down at my computer and arrived at the second version. He found his own way of solving the problems I had pointed out. He also had some ideas about how to tell the rest of his story.

One of the things we discussed at length was the fact that in the original passage he was so busy *describing* things that he had forgotten the need to *demonstrate*. The revision indicates placement of a scene that will show what it is about Nyla that fascinates the narrator. As things *happen* to the characters in a living scene, the author—and readers—will get to know Nyla considerably better.

Nyla was so secure in her self-love that her sense of self simply transcended all other things.    She was so comfortable with ~~loving herself,~~ that ~~her self-love was in no way compromised by~~ loving someone else. She would tell you she loved you, if she actually did; but never ~~could you~~ expect ~~that~~ her love for you would influence the way ~~that~~ she ~~might act~~. Nyla's behavior was solely the function of her first priority - Nyla.    This is not to say that Nyla's ego was so pure that she was ~~void of any~~ vanity -- such would be a lie:  However, Nyla's vanity was more an indiscretion than a flaw.    I mean by this, that her vanities could no more compromise her happiness than could anything else. The green girl was the type of person who could tell you straight out and directly to your face that she was going to hurt you and that she was going to end up screwing you; the type of person who meant it; and the type of person that you believed when they said

18

it.  She was the one person out of a hundred for whom the ultra serious worked; speeches that would have seemed ~~mellow dramatic~~ coming from the other ninety-nine, ~~sounded serious~~ ~~took on a sense of gravity~~ ~~when they were spoken by Nyla.~~  And when she would tell you that she was going to end up hurting you - and you wouldn't for a moment doubt her and you would in fact begin to fear the moment ~~as she spoke of it~~ - you wouldn't be repelled ~~from her~~.  With an hypnotic ~~type of~~ aura that only a vampire should possess, she would effortlessly suck you into your own doom as though it were your God given fate.

As we sat down together so he could work on this passage, my student watched the prose change for the better. As he worked on perfecting the way he said what he had to say, it became clearer to him and to the reader what he was doing. Cleaning up his prose, trying to make it more precise and direct, he made his meaning clearer. Rewriting, he kept the best of what he had done, tightened and gave it direction.

Now let's look at his revision, the result of a single session.

Nyla was so secure in her self-love that her sense of self simply transcended everything else. She was so comfortable with it that loving someone else was not a compromise. She would tell you she loved you, if she actually did, but you couldn't expect her love for you to influence the way she acted. Nyla's acts were the function of what was most important to her—Nyla. This is not to say that she was without vanity—that would be a lie; it was more of an indiscretion than a flaw.

Here, the author leaves space for a scene. He knows he's going to have to DRAMATIZE and DEMONSTRATE to bring Nyla to the reader.

He's already simplified the prose—and in the process, focused on what he's trying to say about Nyla.

She was the one person out of a hundred for whom the ultra serious worked; speeches that would have seemed melodramatic coming from the other 99, sounded serious when she made them. And when she would tell you that she was going to end up hurting you—and you wouldn't for a moment doubt her and you would in fact begin to fear the moment as she spoke of it—you wouldn't be repelled. With an hypnotic aura that only a vampire should possess, she would effortlessly suck you into your own doom as though it was your God-given fate.

This piece has a few more yards to go, but the difference between the author's first and second drafts is dramatic. He's on the right road; if he keeps working, he's going to find a way to interest an audience in his story.

In a way, starting work on a new draft is easier for beginners than for established writers, because:

1. A professional's first version is likely to look fine, even when the author or editor thinks it's off the mark.
2. Most professionals release only work that has already been through several revisions.

Going back to the drawing board can often be painful, but essential. Approached about this book, novelist and critic Thomas M. Disch (*Camp Concentration*, *The Businessman: A Tale of Terror*) was in the process of quitting two jobs in order to get to the revision of a new novel—work he has to do before it's ready to be published. He confessed that he'd been putting off this revision for two years—taking on extra reviewing chores, teaching, writing an interactive computer game—anything to avoid doing what he knew needed doing. Now he's getting down to it.

The knowledge that revision has worked for him before—and will work again—will keep him going. He knows he has to go the last mile to reach his audience. In the process, he will complete the work to his own satisfaction because the best writers are their own harshest critics.

Disch's notebook pages—and final copy of a published story—demonstrate that professionals don't think they're finished even when the work looks finished. Unlike student work, in which flaws are often apparent, his rough draft looks perfectly acceptable. Only the writer knows there's more to be done here. Disch is editing himself even in the first draft, scrawled into a notebook. In the final draft, he has expanded and developed in some cases, cutting back dialogue for effect in some places and in others, punching it up for emphasis.

A look at Disch's manuscript and other samples included in the Appendix demonstrates what a number of working professionals go through on the way to completing a work of fiction.

For the moment, so you can see how the process looks, let's examine just one writer's manuscript pages. Unlike some writers, who use notebooks only when they're away from home, novelist Lois Gould leaves home in order to work in notebooks. She composed her newest novel, *Subject to Change*, in notebooks.

Gould says an early editor quoted the poet, Valery, on revision: "No work of art is ever completed, it is only abandoned."

For her, as for so many other successful writers, revision is part of composition. It is slow, thorough and rewarding. Gould wrote her new novel and made heavy revisions in one set of notebooks. Then she copied the text into another set, revising as she went. This necessitated a third handwritten copy, which then went to a typist. Gould did another revision on the typescript, which was then corrected and sent to her publisher. She admits that she did further revision in galleys, and has made one or two essential word changes in page proofs, the final stage the author sees before receiving bound copies.

She says, "A publisher once said I would end up revising in some bookstore, snatching the last copy out of a customer's hand, muttering, 'Excuse me, sir, I just thought of a better word. Or two . . .?' "

Attached are a notebook page *from the second draft*, along with corresponding page proofs.

He will test it now, upon his own body. The screw can be controlled; a gentle sliding, a flowering within.

his body rising with it, but does not fall.

+ Feb it
just break

Cornelius has unwrapped his magical plant-root; in an excellent he has bathed it
now he sits gazing at it, touching it with a trembling finger. invulnerable
in battle, deadly assuredly in the use of weapons, yet the shape of it
the way its limbs disturbs him; it seems to twist like a woman writhing. In pain, in ecstasy?
And its peculiar yellow, more corpse-like than now, by the candlelight of his candle
then when he first unearthed it? It sweats, or his palms have made it slippery
He covers the thing in its finery; the root
him in the dark recesses of his wardrobe he gazed a plaything: the heretic's
Hard to the touch. a soothing murmur escapes his throat,
pear, the pincers of it. He strokes from this agitation
surprising him. He must rest yet able his
the pear
gleams up at him, as though it would speak. He sets it with the screw
light fingers; springs open silent + powerful. He closes his eyes,
his own breath; the smaller pear will do for another
test, in the morning, he will share it with the king before the jousting
He will spread a salve,
all tasted immost, when the q. red last examined
Brother to brother. Flowering within. slight to sire. guarding grasping its treachery

the queen's precious bedspread, strewn with pearls like
a sunlit sky, lies in a tattered heap upon the floor. Pearls roll
everywhere, the room is
a forest of frightened animals. False! all false! The queen's
on velvet sleeps within golden casket serpent
worthless fancy. This day Catherine has examined her treasures
catalogs, compiled her
riches, There is no doubt
of the thievery. The woman has been questioned, and
the treasurers
Catherine cannot dispel a certain image, the sound of a pearl crashing
upon a marble floor; Cornelius the necromancer
hovering over the queen his hands white rigid, holding
as though they held a casket of magical air, of holy spirit, over her entranced
body. Pearl, how came it there, why falling whence? Cornelius
look, Catherine will to dispel the moment
Nor she reflects upon the crowd of mourners, armourers, magnificent
in the stalls. Cornelius + Henry,

gician, he must not know the truth of the contest until after he wins it.

SAFE IN HIS ROOMS, Cornelius has unwrapped his magical plant-root, bathed it in an excellent wine, fed it with hearty rough bread. Now he sits gazing at it, touching it with a lover's trembling fingertip. Invulnerable in battle, deadly aim in the use of weapons . . . yet the shape of it disturbs him still. arousing a feeling of dread, like a sickness. It is the way its limbs seem to twist, like the limbs of a woman, grotesque, writhing. In pain or ecstasy? Are they one and the same, in a woman? Is the peculiar yellow color of the thing more corpse-like now, by the light of his candle, than when he first unearthed it? Does it sweat, or do his own moist palms make it slip in his grasp? Quaking now, he wraps the hideous thing in its finery, his fingers fumbling with the strips of cloth, leaving it half exposed. He flings open his wardrobe, thrusts the root deep within it, gropes for a safer plaything to occupy his restless hand, and finds it. Hard, cool to the touch, polished: an iron pear. It is a torture instrument of remarkable beauty. He strokes its rounded flanks; a soothing moan escapes his throat, surprising him. He must rest from this agitation he suffers, yet his senses rise. The black pear gleams up at him, as though it would speak. He tests its stem, within which lies the concealed screw; he turns it; the fruit springs open at his command, its perfect crescents silent and powerful, capable of shattering a mouth, teeth, jaws; or the inmost parts of a man or woman. He

it, but does not fall. Why not test the pear, now, upon his own body? The screw can be easily controlled, a gentle insertion of the pear, a sliding, a flowering within; no harm done. If all goes well he will share this fruit with the king. He prepares an unguent now, a salve. Yes. If all goes well, he will share this fruit with the king. Before the jousting. Brother to brother. Knight to sire. Flowering within.

THE QUEEN'S PRECIOUS BEDSPREAD, strewn with pearls like the night sky, lies in a tattered heap upon the floor. Pearls roll and scatter in all directions, white eyes darting into dark corners, until the hushed chamber is a forest filled with frightened animals. False! All false! The queen's fabled rope, coiled upon its velvet cushion, sleeps within its golden casket, guarding its treachery like the serpent in Paradise. A worthless forgery. This day a trusted serving woman, inspired by the lady Diane, inquired, all innocent, when the queen had last examined her treasures; when summoned the catalogues, the records? At once the queen commanded a counting, a recounting, a weighing and a balancing of every relic, every jewel.

There is no doubt of the thievery. The serving woman has been interrogated; all the serving women. The treasurers themselves; a hundred guards and grooms. Catherine cannot dispel a certain image, the sound of a single pearl crashing, rolling upon a marble floor; Cornelius the necromancer hovers over the queen, his white hands poised, rigid, as though they held a priceless gift of magical air,

Yes the notebook pages are hard—almost impossible—to read. For this author, recopying to make her changes legible on a new version is part of the revision process. Every time she does this, something changes and the work develops further. Revising, the author is refining word choices, becoming more precise about objects used by the character; she is furthering the development of the scene as she forges the language to create it. Like Disch, Gould is a stylist, whose choice of language fits and creates her subject.

Novelist, historian and biographer Paul Horgan talks compellingly about revision in his book, *Approaches to Writing* (Farrar, Straus and Giroux, 1974; Wesleyan University Press, 1988). The author, who has won two Pulitzer prizes, threw away five novels before he published *Fault of Angels*, which won the Harper Prize. He is a meticulous craftsman, who composes on the typewriter and revises in pencil, moving on to another typescript and yet another revision. He writes:

Revision word by word and sentence does follow, for me, not once, but many times, each for different values.

*These embrace precision in meaning*; as between two words of equal precision, choice, then, of that one which calls up image more vividly through color or sound or association; rhythm, the great key to readability, in small units of the text, such as the phrase and the sentence, rhythm in larger developments of the text, such as paragraph and the chapter, and finally rhythm in the work as a whole. In fiction, revision pursues each character of the story in a separate reading to feel the consistency, the living presence of each. Another complete revision is devoted to an examination to improve atmosphere and background. And so on, paying attention to each of the elements, including the humble mechanics, which combine to make a finished work—such matters as simple correctness in spelling, punctuation, grammar, syntax—the technical fabric by which the rich English language, with all its tributaries, is given its primary power of communication.

. . . Such elements as I speak of are the structural fibers of writing, and not to respect them for their own sake, and to love their purposes and their powers, is to have little promise as a writer.

The italics are mine. They demonstrate an important point about both writing and revision: *We find out what we have to say as we decide how to say it.*

As he reads for rhythm and precision, Horgan's revision develops and organizes what he has to say—*as he works on the way in which he says it.*

If words are the stuff out of which fiction is made, writers need—even in the early stages—to find THE RIGHT ONES. Having completed a draft *the best way we know how, using the best possible materials* from the very beginning, we still need to be careful, critical readers. There is more to be done.

I believe something profound happens to us when we begin revising. Two recent studies of manuscripts and working papers of famous American writers demonstrate.

In his introduction to *Faulkner's Revision of Absalom, Absalom!* Gerald Langford writes:

> As one of the major achievements in twentieth-century fiction, William Faulkner's *Absalom, Absalom!* would be an instructive work in which to study the writer's revisions even if these were confined to matters of word choice and sentence structure. Some of the revisions, however, are structural, and it is particularly interesting to learn that, while writing and reworking the novel, Faulkner altered in several ways his original design. . . . To trace the process of such revision is to experience a sharp focusing of the dominant theme of the novel, and to witness a demonstration of how the meaning of a fictional work can shape its structure and thus stand revealed by what has become the outward and visible sign, or form, of that meaning.

By making a close study of all the working papers of this famous American author, Langford has hit upon and demonstrated the truth of revision. Writers who have the time and patience would do well to look up this University of Texas Press book, which walks the reader through all the stages of Faulkner's struggle with his material. You see the novel develop under the author's hands *as he revises.*

Beginning *The Great Gatsby*, F. Scott Fitzgerald wrote:

"I want to write something *new* — something extraordinary and beautiful and simple + intricately patterned."

He did it at last, but not before throwing out one version of what he was trying to say and starting over from a "new angle." Completing a new draft, he then wrote: "Hard work sets in." He was talking about revision. Once a typist had taken over, he made more changes on what scholar/biographer Matthew J. Bruccoli believes were multiple typescripts.

Bruccoli examines the process in his introduction to a book containing photocopies of Fitzgerald's heavily revised original manuscript (*The Great Gatsby, A Facsimile of the Manuscript,* Microcard Editions Books). In those days of cheaper composition costs, Fitzgerald made further revisions for editor Maxwell Perkins in the final typescript and completed them in galley proofs. He later wrote: "Max, it amuses me when praise comes in on the 'structure' of the book — because it was you who fixed up the structure, not me." What "fixed up" the structure was Fitzgerald's willingness to continue revision even after the book had been contracted for.

The book he is talking about is his acknowledged masterpiece.

These established writers' drafts demonstrate what to me seems the most important aspect of the process of revision, which cannot be separated from the process of composition. Again, we need to remember, because it is essential to everything we as writers do: *We find out what we have to say even as we are perfecting our ways of saying it.*

This dramatic strengthening of the writer's powers of DEVELOPMENT and ORGANIZATION is the magical gift revision brings to the writer who has the wits and courage to spend the time on it.

This, then, is the hidden payoff of revision, and the strongest single reason I can think of for anybody who hopes to be a writer to write fiction with the idea that the first version is only the first step on what may be a long, hard road with success at the end.

Knowing what you do now about how established professionals think about their work, ask yourself:

1. When I write, do I try to say exactly what I mean?

2. Am I trying to put down the best thing I have to say in *the best way I can say it?*

3. Do I do this every time, or am I sometimes hasty or careless?

Asking yourself this question, remember that if you don't care about what you're doing, there's no reason any reader should. Your readers are going to get out of this work *only what you put into it.*

4. Am I heading in the right direction?

Remember, a wrong turn is a wrong turn, whether you take it at the very beginning of a story or in the later stages. A wrong choice made early in a piece of work can throw the entire mechanism out of kilter. Ask yourself: *Even in a first draft* can I try harder to find:

    a. The right name for the person or object I'm naming?
    b. The exact verb?
    c. The fresh and accurate adjective?

5. Am I willing to slow down enough to do these things in order to make my intentions clear to my reader?

You may already think you're trying hard in all these categories, and doing pretty well—you probably are. This book is designed to help you do even better.

Once you're committed to doing your absolute best *from the moment you sit down to write*, you're ready for a more detailed approach to revision.

# CHAPTER 3

---

# KINDS OF REVISION

YOU MAY BE RELIEVED TO KNOW that there is no right way or wrong way to write or revise fiction. Manuscript samples in the preceding chapter and in the Appendix demonstrate this.

Even moving by at high speeds, you can see that there are almost as many ways of going at revision as there are writers. Every good writer reads for style, character, truth of dialogue and accuracy of detail. These organic parts of the process of revision follow naturally from what I think of as the first two major kinds of revision:

1. *Draft writing, draft revision.* The draft writer gets out a first draft without stopping to look back and make changes. Revision comes in subsequent drafts.

2. *Block construction,* or: *revising as you go.* The writer using block construction revises sentence by sentence, progressing slowly through a story or novel to what is essentially a polished version.

Add to these first two major kinds of revision, a third. This one takes place after the story or novel exists in more or less complete form. It is:

3. *Revision to strengthen structure and story.* Reading for story, character, shape and what to put in and what to leave out, you may think you've already done this. Then it's time to read the work one more time—and do it again, if you have to. This involves an overall look at what appears to be a finished manuscript. It comes after all those considerations of style, character,

truth of dialogue and accuracy of detail are completed. This third kind of revision comes *after you think you're finished*.

Because they're part of the process of composition, we'll begin with the first two methods of revision.

Most writers use a combination of these first two methods. Draft writers are making word choices and phrase selections even as they move through the first draft, finding story and establishing structure. Sentence draft writers will perfect each sentence and each paragraph as they move on to the end of what looks like a finished and completely polished version, but then go back to do fine-tuning and in some cases find themselves making a structural revision.

Whichever method you use, you need to remember: AMONG PROFESSIONALS, REVISION IS PART AND PARCEL OF COMPOSING.

## I. DRAFT WRITING, DRAFT REVISION

Some writers get their stories down *fast*, writing a rough draft while the idea is hot. They do their revising and fine-tuning on their second draft, their third, their eighth. They want to see the whole story so they can work with it.

Novelist and short story writer C.E. Poverman, whose first collection won the Iowa School of Letters Award for Short Fiction, quotes William Saroyan on this: "Something is better than nothing." Even if it's imperfect by nature, the first draft is a beginning.

*A rough draft gives you a place to start.*

It's far more productive to have a draft to work with—however faulty—than to sit staring at a blank page or a blank screen because our self-confidence is shaky, or because we're determined that the first sentence of the first page we write must be perfect.

This is particularly important to writers who can't get started because they can't bear to put down anything that isn't perfect. We all know so-called perfectionists who brood endlessly over a pocket full of ideas or the same handful of pages, letting us know that they are sitting on the greatest work on earth—if it ever gets finished. They may think they are perfectionists but they're only fooling themselves; they're putting off getting started.

Until you have something on the page, you aren't really writing fiction, you're only talking about it.

Remember, *nothing you write is carved in stone*. Draft writers know better than anybody that a faulty version of a story or novel is better than no version at all, and they know better than anybody that the first draft gives them something concrete that will improve as they work on it. They get down their ideas in a draft that from the beginning is designed to be rewritten. Thus: *first draft*.

A first draft is a starting place. *Once it's out there, we can do anything we want with it.*

Humorist James Thurber put it another way: "Don't get it right, get it written."

## Survival Tactics

Some draft writers like to make a distinction between drafts by the methods they use to put their work on paper. It gives them the sense that they are making progress. Some will start with a notebook, composing by hand. When the notebook gets too hard to read, they let a typist make a clean copy so they can enter further changes by hand.

It cheers them up to see the first hesitant pages with scrawled notes and crossings-out replaced by a clean typescript. The progression to each new stage is a big milestone.

Others begin writing by hand and for the second draft, go directly to the typewriter or the computer. People who compose on typewriter or computer will choose different kinds of ink or paper to mark the progress from one draft to the next, or move from dot matrix to letter quality printer—anything to mark progress.

Advancing to a second draft, the draft writer goes back to correct the first and sometimes sketchy version, and to expand on it. Suggested descriptions take a fuller form. Hastily sketched scenes develop into full-blown dramatic moments. New scenes develop. The story organizes itself.

## Advantages of Draft Writing

1. The psychological trick—thinking "it's only a draft"—makes it easier to get started. Think of a runner or a swimmer warming up. We've all got to write that first page sometime, and for many draft writers, the first draft is a warmup.

2. First drafts are often like first loves—vivid and passionate. The draft writer manages to enjoy all of the pleasure and excitement that come with a new idea, the delight that comes with invention. They are at the very beginning of the long road between first thought and finished product. The skilled draft writer manages to keep a sense of this first energy and passion in subsequent, more detailed and more fully developed versions.

3. A draft is an efficient way to find out where the story is going. Once the first draft is finished, you have the entire story in front of you. There are the bare bones of the idea more or less outlined, along with some of those inspired moments—the paragraphs or scenes that make it directly from the world of inspiration and onto the page without running out of control in the process.

4. The writer with a finished first draft knows where the story has been and where it's going. The first draft lets you see the entire story, from beginning to end—how it starts and what happens. *Because you know how the story comes out*, it's possible to go back to the beginning and make everything point toward the inevitable ending. Revising, you have the advantage of foresight and hindsight.

5. Early drafts by a true draft writer are the place for experiments and adventures, hits and easily forgiven misses. The investment of time is not as great as it will be when you reach the "final" draft, and rewrites are not as daunting. This is, after all, only a draft you are working on.

Writing in *The New York Times Book Review*, short story writer

David Huddle underlines the importance of recognizing a draft for what it is—something written on the way to what you are really writing. He talks about esthetic luck, suggesting that, like athletes, writers have good days and bad days:

> Esthetic luck is the major argument in favor of working through a process of revising a piece of writing though many drafts. If you're a supremely talented artist and you hit a very lucky day, then maybe you can write a poem or story or chapter of a novel that needs no revision. If you're a regular writer with your appointed portion of esthetic luck, you'll need to come at the piece again and again. I like to think of revision as a form of self-forgiveness; you can allow yourself mistakes and shortcomings in your writing because you know you're coming back later to improve it. Revision is the way you cope with the bad luck that made your writing less than brilliant this morning. Revision is the hope you hold out for yourself to make something beautiful tomorrow though you didn't quite manage it today.

6. The time scheme—how long it takes between writing the first page of one draft and beginning the next one—allows leeway for second thoughts, further development. You can think about changes, make further notes. Many draft writers make large organizational changes between drafts. Others discover that the story develops more fully and sometimes changes significantly between drafts. Think of time-lapse photographs of a child—at infancy, three, five, eight. It's the same child, but bigger and more fully developed. A child grows and changes. So will your manuscript.

## II. BLOCK CONSTRUCTION: REVISING AS YOU GO

Having said all that about the advantages of draft writing, I wonder why I proceed the way I do—the way so many other writers do—perfecting each sentence, each paragraph and each page before going on to the next one.

I'll call what we do *block construction*.

I happened into block construction because I'm an essentially lazy person. Remember those sixty-six busted stories. The idea of writing a first draft *and then writing the whole thing all over* seemed horrible to me. Think of all that trouble! Think of all that time spent on making a new draft, copying the thing over in order to make changes. I used to think of it as time wasted.

If I could only get a story right the first time, I thought, I wouldn't have to rewrite it. I could spend my life avoiding revision.

Impatient by nature, I was never meant to be a draft writer. Instead, drawing on the experience of my newspaper days, I decided to shortstop criticism by making my first draft as right as I could make it. Composing on the typewriter, I was willing to type and retype and keep retyping my beginning *until I had it absolutely right*.

Clever me. No rewrites for me, I thought. My first draft is my only draft. Never mind how long it takes me to reach the end of it. Remember, this was the act of a lazy person.

Because I was convinced I was avoiding work by taking more pains at the beginning, I was happy to type and retype and retype a page *of my only draft*; I was willing to spend just as long on it as I had to spend to make it right, just as long as I thought when I wrote "the end" I was really going to be finished.

It's only now, as I remember the cartons upon cartons of working papers I piled up that I see how I managed to fool myself. Thinking I was taking the easy way out, I moved naturally into the essential habit of hard work. Discarded sentence and page drafts show me exactly how hard I worked then—how hard I'm still working. At the time it seemed natural and logical. It still does. Perhaps the key to the success of block construction is logic.

## Sentence Draft Writers Begin at the Beginning

Reporters say that once you have your lead, your story is written. It seemed to me that if I could get my first sentence right, I would have my story in hand. I wrote and rewrote the first sen-

tence until the second unrolled more or less naturally. I worked
on the first paragraph until I had it right before moving on to
the second. I perfected the first page before moving on to the
next.

Something interesting happened along the way. If I made
a word change or even a typing error on a page I would pull it
out of the typewriter and start retyping it. Every time I did this,
something happened. Sometimes I ended up reorganizing a
paragraph I hadn't even realized needed it; other times I would
find the story had taken its next logical turn, or a character
would demonstrate depths I hadn't known were there the first
time I wrote the scene. In the course of rewriting and re-rewrit-
ing (who was I fooling? I was never just retyping), in the course
of improving the way I told my story, I made discoveries about
it. My story developed as I forged the telling.

I was figuring out what I had to say as I found the right way
to say it. From character names to setting details to precise
nouns and exact verbs, word choices determine the course of
fiction. Let me give you some idea how this happens.

Computer freaks play a game called *Zork*, the granddaddy
of interactive computer games. The first screen gives minimal
information. You are standing in a field. There is a mailbox next
to you; in one direction there is a house; in another, a forest.
You must decide which way to go. The next stage of the story
reveals itself as you make your initial choices.

At every stage, making a choice uncovers more story and
reveals a new batch of options.

If you choose the house, and find the trap door under the
rug in the living room, you are let into a vast underground
labyrinth. At each step you are presented with new choices. Go
one way and you may be killed by the troll. Go another and
you are on your way to discovering uncounted underground
treasures. You must consider each choice carefully because each
offers a different set of options.

Move slowly, choose carefully and you'll discover the extent
of the underground kingdom. You may even survive to come
back aboveground with all those treasures.

In a way, as writers, we are all exploring unknown territory.

Choose this narrative point of view and those characters and you've already decided a number of things about your story. You are developing narrative options. Block construction makes us make these choices *in order* and slows the rate at which we make them. Perfecting sentence by sentence, building block by block narrows the margin for error, as you choose among your options. Correct choices will lead you to the right ending for the piece of fiction you are writing.

I'm not the only writer who works this way. If you look at the drafts reproduced in the Appendix, you'll see that each of these writers is in an individual way refining and improving on what is on the page before moving on. And in each case the payoff is developmental.

## Advantages to Block Construction

1. In some ways, commitment to sentence drafts is liberating. It allows us to play psychological tricks on ourselves in some of the ways draft writers do when they establish milestones by changing from pen or pencil to keyboard, or from one to another kind of paper.

a. It's easy to get to work because I don't have to write the whole story or chapter today. I don't even have to write a whole page. All I have to do is get one or two good sentences. If things don't go well today, I won't die because I also know there's some kind of buildup of energy. Ideas develop overnight. As long as I have something on the page, it's going to get better tomorrow.

b. This isn't a draft. Revision isn't daunting because it doesn't seem so much like revision. We're not talking about recasting a whole novel here, or even a whole story. I'm only rewriting a sentence. Never mind all those cartons of working papers. Perfecting one sentence at a time seems easy because after all, a sentence is only a sentence.

c. I have the advantage of the running head start. If things aren't going well I can always go back and tinker with the last few pages I wrote yesterday. By the time I've done the last bits of housekeeping on yesterday's work, refining this string of words, expanding that one, making narrative decisions as I go, I have a running head start into today's work. I've found out what's going to happen next.

2. Block construction makes writers begin at the beginning. Perfecting a first page, the writer is setting the style and the tone, pace and point of view of what is going to follow. By the time I have written a first page to my satisfaction, I know who is telling or observing the story, what the rhythms are. I am beginning to understand how to write what happens next.

3. As I suggest above, block construction is developmental. Not all of us start with a story completely formed in our heads, just waiting to be transferred to the page. Most of us who write longer fiction are like those computer freaks, playing *Zork*. We have to make choices in order to find out what we know, discovering details about our characters, listening closely to what they have to say to each other. Once we know who these people really *are*, we can find out what's going to happen to them. We know exactly how they're going to respond or react in any given situation.

The work develops naturally, limiting the possibility for characters to act out of character and protecting us from making hasty, sometimes wrong, narrative choices.

4. Block construction gives us time to solve problems as they come up, instead of putting them off for a later draft. All writers are doing work in their heads even when they look as if they aren't working. We walk around carrying unsolved problems in our heads, with our subconscious hard at work on unanswered questions. Building page by page, those of us who work by block construction move on to the next scene only after this one is solid.

5. We're discovering what we have to say. Advancing at the rate of a few paragraphs or a couple of pages a day, we find that much of our work is done in our heads in the hours between the time when we get up from work and the next day when we go back to it. Sometimes this means walking away from a story problem, letting it sit overnight. More often than not, we come back the next day to discover that the problem has solved itself. At other times, notes present themselves in batches. Ideas that were barely hatched on one day are all grown up by the next one.

6. Because we started at the beginning and are building block by block, things happen in order. This gives narrative control: events proceed logically and characters are true to themselves.

Looking at what I've done after a scene has developed, I may have to go back to expand or to cut, to change the shadings in a certain section or to explain a little more. What I don't have to do is go back and change what's happened, or try to wrench characters back on track. Characters who develop naturally behave that way.

## REVISION AS A WAY OF LIFE

I said I began to compose this way, revising as I went, because I am an essentially lazy person who hated the idea of revision. This is particularly interesting to me now in view of all those cartons of working papers, in view of the fact that I can't number the hundreds of changes and corrections I've made even in the process of writing this chapter. It's clear that by trying to second-guess critics and get things right the first time, I backed into revision as a way of life. It is part and parcel of every paragraph I write.

The cold truth, however, is that in spite of all the dozens of stages I go through in composition, I am no better off than draft writers. Like them, when I write "the end," I'm not necessarily finished.

There are questions all of us need to ask ourselves, whether we're sitting down to read a first draft or a manuscript we think is essentially finished:
- Is it a story?
- Does something really happen? Is it going to be clear to the reader?
- If this is a story, is it as good as I can make it? Is it all here or are there key scenes or details missing? Do I need to cut or expand to enhance organization?
- Even though I think it's all here, are the scenes just sketched, or are they fully developed, so the reader will see what I see?

- Does everything unfold in the right order?
- Am I describing, or TELLING, more than I am demonstrating through scenes; i.e., SHOWING?
- Is it too long for what it does?
- If so, where does it need cutting?
- What about the tone? Does the whole thing sound as if it's written by the same person?

Whether you compose through several drafts or work mainly by block construction, so that your first attempt *looks* finished, you need to sit down, *read carefully* and ask yourself all these questions.

## WHAT'S NEXT

As I suggested at the beginning of this chapter, there is no right or wrong way to write or revise fiction. Most of us find the way that's most comfortable for us, and it's likely to be a combination of draft and block writing and revision. No matter which mehod we choose, sooner or later we come up against that moment when we have written "the end" and discover we still need to consider one more reading, for that third major kind of revision: revision to strengthen structure and story.

This raises an important point. *There are things you have to do even after you think you are finished.*

### Reading for Revision to Strengthen Structure and Story

All of us who write for a living take a work as far as we can take it before it leaves our hands. If we are draft writers we've worked through as many drafts as it takes us to arrive at a finished product. If we work by block construction, we've considered and reconsidered at every stage to make our story as good as we can make it. In some cases everything is fine. In others, we're too close to what we've written to see it from the outside.

We need help moving on to the next stage—what I think of as the third major kind of revision. I'm talking about reading with the idea that we may need to make further revisions to strengthen structure and story. This is the final judgment, shaping and in some cases reordering that makes a story or a novel move in a straight line from beginning to end. Whether we compose by draft or put our fiction together block by block, many of us think we've finished a story or a novel when, in fact, it's still not quite right. It may be too long in some places, or underdeveloped in others, or the major sections may be out of order.

We're reading for:

1. Truth of action
2. Accessibility
3. Completeness
4. Time scheme
5. Point of view
6. Length (with an eye to possible cutting)
7. Organization
8. And, once again, balance of showing versus telling.

I'll give you a special checklist and talk about this third major kind of revision at length in Chapter Eight: Reading for Story and Structure.

## Finding Out Whether You're Finished

Meanwhile, it's important to note that most of us need help reaching the point where we're able to make this kind of judgment about a recently finished work. Some of us need to know when to persist. Others need to be told when to quit.

As writers, we've lived inside our story or novel on a day-to-day basis for so long that we're like construction workers with a complete set of blueprints who see only the immediate details of what they're building: how things are put together, what materials they're using. We're too close to our work to be able to see it clearly.

Whether we need to be told to stop or ordered to persist, we all need outside readers. It's time to get away from our work — to walk out of the house of words we have been building so we can stand back and get a good look at it.

This is the only way we're ever going to be able to see what it looks like to others.

We need distance.

## CHAPTER 4

# HOW TO FIND OUT WHETHER YOU'RE FINISHED WHEN YOU THINK YOU'RE FINISHED

YOU'VE JUST FINISHED a story.

How do you feel about it?

Because you've just finished, you may feel all those good things about finishing this piece of work: happy it's over, proud of it, hopeful for its future. You may also feel some not-so-good things—uncertainty as to whether your judgment is objective, that nagging suspicion that readers aren't going to see what you see, that your piece may not be all there yet.

You recognize the need for revision in an abstract way, but remember, you've just finished this story you're so proud of. How are you supposed to know whether it needs revision?

You may think it's the best thing you've done so far and it may be, but is it as good as you think it is? Is it as good as you can make it? Some wit pointed out that even a skunk smells like a gardenia to its mother.

Remember, some writers need to be told to persist, while others need to be told when to quit.

If you'd rather start something new than improve what you have, you belong in the first category.

If you'd rather go back than go forward, you belong in the second. Many beginning writers get so committed to process that they forget they're on the way to a finished manuscript—a piece of work they can walk away from with a sense of pride and accomplishment. They'd rather brood over a manuscript, cherish it and fuss with tiny changes than begin something new or find out what other people think of what they've written. Compulsive tinkering helps them maintain the illusion that they're writers without ever having to do what professionals do:

1. Finish.
2. Lay it on the line and have it judged by others.

They tell themselves and others that they're *on the way to something perfect* when in fact they're not going anywhere.

They're protecting their sensitive feelings and putting off the inevitable hard work that comes with starting something new. These compulsive revisers make endless insignificant changes because it gives them the illusion that they're working while protecting them from the moment of truth.

If you are inclined to tinker, you may need to be ruthless with yourself. Set a limit to the number of drafts you will write before you put your story aside and/or *get an outside reading*.

Which kind of writer are you?

Whether you find it too easy to quit—or too hard—you're going to have to ask yourself a few hard questions.

1. Have I taken this piece of work as far as I can take it?
2. Have I made everything clear or am I leaving too much to my reader's imagination?
3. How does it stack up against other stories of its kind?

Now, how are you going to know the answers? It's time to distance yourself. You can do this in several ways.

## SEEING YOUR STORY AS A WHOLE

There are three ways in which writers learn what stories are shaped like, and find out how to tell whether a particular story is in working order. You will learn:

1. By writing so many stories that you as writer know *from*

*the inside* what stories are shaped like and how they work. If you write enough stories over enough years, you'll see this for yourself. If you're willing to be flexible about when to revise—and when to quit. If you keep at it long enough, you will eventually develop the professional's *sense of rightness*. This is the click—as if of a camera's shutter—that lets you know the picture is complete. Part of the business of this book is to help you to write, and write enough so that you can find out what stories feel like *from the inside*. It's one of the best ways to find out whether they're in working condition.

2. Through reading.

3. Through distancing.

4. With the help of outside readers.

## BACKGROUND IN READING

Writers probably ought to spend as much time reading fiction as they do on their own writing.

To answer questions about your own work honestly and accurately, you need some basis for comparison—a sense of what the competition is like, and what the winners are doing. I'm assuming that if you want to write fiction and care about what you're doing, you already do a lot of reading.

You need to read as widely as you can, to have such a broad background in fiction that you escape the danger of focusing on one writer or one particular style of writing and getting trapped writing second-rate imitation. If you read hundreds of stories, dozens of novels, you'll develop a built-in sense of form—what good fiction looks like to the reader. If you know what *hundreds* of short stories look like, then you begin to develop a sense of what makes a good short story. You're not doing this in order to imitate. Instead you're finding out what fiction is about by reading as much as you can make time for.

The same is true of longer fiction.

If you know what kind of a writer you are—mainstream or science fiction or romance or mystery, it makes sense to read a lot of the specific *kind* of thing you think you are writing, everything from acknowledged classics to what's being published this year. Reading work by new writers, you're going to come up against their successes and failures. Judging their work, you'll know better how to judge your own.

In a way, it's like judging show dogs. You have to know what the *best* Scottie looks like before you can tell whether or not you have a good one. Yours may be adorable, but unless he measures up, he's not going to qualify for the show.

As a writer and not a Scottie trainer, you have a major advantage: *You can be as original as you like as long as your fiction succeeds in its own terms.*

Reading widely and writing extensively, you will begin to develop a sense of whether or not a story is working. Notice what characterizes traditional stories, with beginnings, middles, ends—and how far experimental writers go in nontraditional stories. The sky's the limit AS LONG AS THE STORY IS WORKING. If you write enough stories, you will develop the *insider's sense of rightness.* Judging the work of professionals, from the authors of acknowledged masterpieces to contemporary fiction, you'll begin to see when stories work for you, and when they don't. This helps you set standards for your own fiction. You'll know when your own stories are working. As you gain confidence, you can begin to explore and experiment. Remember, you can do anything you want in a story as long as it works.

## DISTANCING

If you've done everything you can with a story—taken it through several drafts—and you're doubtful about whether this piece is a success or not, and how you feel about it, you're still too close. You may need help moving out of the story or novel you've built so you can see it from the outside.

You're going to want to find out:

1. Whether it's really finished.
2. Whether it works.
3. Whether after your revisions, it still needs revision.
4. Which parts need work.

5. What to do.
6. How to go about it.

You're going to get specific suggestions for revising in chapters to come, but right now we're talking about how you, as writer, can find out what about your work may need revising.

It's time to distance yourself so you can make some harsh judgments.

First we'll talk about informal distancing. There are a couple of ways to do this. For many of us, the first is the hardest.

1. *Put it away for a while.* My resident critic calls this letting the lasagna set before you serve it. A few days, or weeks, or months of distance from the actual writing of your story give your pulse and heartbeat time to return to normal. If it was love at first sight, a second look may change your mind.

By the time you return to the piece of work you were so proud of, the first fine flush of romance will have given way to the clearer light of reality.

Faults are going to be easier to spot. Gaps and missing links will be more apparent. Things you as writer knew but failed to tell the reader are going to show up because in time, you'll finally be able to forget what you knew as writer and start to function as reader. The flush of inspiration gives way to the harsh light of a critical reading. You may even find yourself saying, "I can't believe I did that."

Unfortunately, most of us hate to *lose the time*. We have a hard time putting away work we think is finished. We're pleased to be finished and a little proud. There's no fun in having a new toy if we can't show it to the other kids. More important, we're anxious to find out whether others like it as much as we do.

2. If you can't stand to put it away, then *read it aloud*.

a. To yourself. Reading aloud gives you another kind of distance from what you've written. Those words are no longer private things, secrets kept between you and the page. Instead they're rolling around in the room. Klunky prose and untrue dialogue become particularly apparent in this kind of reading.

b. To somebody else. This kind of reading aloud is excruciating for most of us and extremely productive. In addition to hearing that klunky prose and untrue dialogue *along with* the listener, you're going to become painfully aware of boring stretches—things that go on too long for what they do, dramatic moments that don't come off, missing links or gaps in the narrative. If you've done your work well, there's also the possibility for instant gratification—the gasp at what horrifies, laughter at what's funny.

## OUTSIDE READERS

Let's say you've done some or all these things. If you've read this piece of work aloud to a patient listener, you've already moved into phase two: audience. Let's say you're sensitive; if anybody says a harsh word, you're going to die. One of the first things you're going to need to learn as writer is how to *not die*. This means learning how to subject your work to scrutiny and take criticism as calmly as possible. Nobody is going to like your work as well as you do, but your work doesn't have much of a life for itself until somebody else reads it.

Remember, unless you're a closet writer, writing for yourself with no intention of letting anybody else see what you've done, eventually you're going to run up against the outside reader. You can call the shots, however, by deciding whether to try your work out on a trusted friend or a teacher or, at the formal level, by submitting it to an editor or magazine. Although there are dozens of possible ways to get readings, there are three routes to an audience:

1. Informal readings.
2. Workshop or classroom setting.
3. Hitting the front line—aiming for publication.

### *One-on-One Readings*

If you opt for individual, or one-on-one readings, there may be questions you can ask your readers—trusted friends, mates, relatives. Since informal situations are sensitive at best and depend heavily on your relationship with the person you've asked to read, you'll have to feel your way to some extent, tailoring questions according to the story in question. Because no two stories—or readers—are alike, there are no hard-and-fast rules on this one. Some of these attitudes, however, can also help you in workshop or classroom. When getting one-on-one readings, remember:

1. You may be feeling fragile, but this is a sensitive situation for your reader, too. If a negative response is going to ruin your friendship, find a reader who has less at stake.
2. Try to leave your reader alone with your work. If you're rattling around the room or hanging over your reader's shoulder, you're not going to get as close a reading as you'd like.
3. Don't prejudice your reader. Hold comments and questions until the end.
4. Don't go fishing for praise. Be direct: "What do you think?"
5. After you get the reader's general impression, ask for details.

Let's assume your reader did not respond with a standing ovation. There are things you want to know. Base specific questions on:

a. What your reader just said. If there are things your reader likes, you'll want to know what they are. If your reader thinks there are problems, keep talking until you have the details—what the reader thinks are problems, why and where.

b. Your own questions about the manuscript. Now is the time to raise any doubts you may have about whether your story's all there, whether your reader sees what you were trying to say, whether individual scenes are working, whether you've done what you set out to do—write something funny or dramatic or suspenseful or frightening. Now's the time to ask, "Did you get so-and-so?" "Is it too. . ."

## Be a Good Listener

Perhaps the most important thing you need to know in putting your work before an audience—even your mom—is that you're

going to get a response, and the response is not always going to
be positive. With this in mind, there are several important things
to know about getting a reading, beginning with how to listen
to criticism. The attitudes toward criticism you form in one-on-
one readings will help you in group situations.

1. Keep an open mind. You asked for this reading. Unless
you listen to the response, the effort is wasted.

2. Don't expect applause. If you get it, naturally you're going to be delighted, but if you expect to use this reader more
than once, you're going to have to ask for complete honesty and
be grateful, not angry, when you get it.

3. Don't expect specific suggestions for rewriting. Remember, readings are for diagnostic purposes. Expect your reader
to point out problems, not to solve them. It's enough for your
reader to say something makes sense or doesn't, or works or
doesn't. It's up to you to figure out what to do about it.

4. If you get specific suggestions, remember: readers aren't
always right. Take what advice you can use and reserve judgment on the rest. Sort out what you can use from what you can't
use. No reader is likely to be right on target about *every single
thing*. Complaints or suggestions are useful at pinpointing *symptoms*. Don't count on your reader to supply the cure.

5. Don't argue. It makes more sense to stand back and reconsider than to use up good time defending what you've written. Even when you think your reader is wrong about something, you're not going to gain anything by arguing. Argument
wastes time and alienates your reader. If you fight to the mat
with a reader over comments on something you've done, trying
to force a change of mind, you're going to lose your reader.

6. Be constructive, not defensive. Look at this in a work-
manlike way: If these are my reader's objections, what can I do
to my story to make it readerproof?

7. Don't act hurt, either. If you think you're going to be a
professional, you're going to have to learn how to be professional in your responses. You asked for an honest opinion, and
whether or not you like what you got, you're going to have to
act grateful for the time the reader spent on you.

8. Keep the lines of communication open. If you get a negative response, ASK QUESTIONS. Remember, you're pinpointing symptoms. Questions can often help you locate the source of a reader's objections. When this happens, discussion can help you figure out what's *really* wrong, and how to fix it.

9. If you're doubtful about recommendations you get from your first reader, get a second opinion. You'd do this if you were going in for surgery. In a way, this is the same thing. You're trying to find out whether there's anything the matter with the patient, so you can decide what to do for it. If you think you may have to perform surgery on what you've written, it's logical to get a second opinion.

With these general rules in mind, it's time to look for your audience. Here are some ways to go about it, beginning with the one-on-one readings that will help you learn to live with criticism.

1. *Getting informal readings.* Give the work you think is finished to a trusted reader. Most of us are lucky enough to have somebody to try our work out on—the dress rehearsal for friends before the show goes on before a more critical audience. This trusted reader may be a teacher you had in high school or college who is still interested in your work and willing to read it, a fellow writer or a member of the family. Some people like to give work to three or more readers, sending out several copies of a book or story at a time to compare responses so they can triangulate. Because this reader is somebody you know personally, pay special attention to the rules for being a good listener. Friendships or relationships are at stake here. If you can't get along with your first reader, find another one.

2. *Workshop or classroom setup.* Not everybody has a friend, relative, colleague or present or former teacher with solid literary judgment. For people in most cities, towns and communities, there are other ways to get your work read and discussed on a relatively informal basis. There are people out there who are interested in the same things you are.

In ascending order of focus, demand for commitment and effectiveness, these include:

a. The informal writing group. Some people like to find others interested in writing, who meet to share work and exchange opinions. These groups are usually made up of beginning writers, which means they may not be as far along in what they're doing as you are. As most writers, particularly beginning writers, usually criticize fiction in terms of what they themselves like to write, they're likely to think you should solve your problems the way they solve their problems. The difficulty, then, is taking the criticism for what it's worth, considering the source in each case.

Like all groups, however, the informal writing group fulfills a key function. If you show your piece to eight people in a group and seven out of eight don't get it, chances are you have a problem.

b. The writing workshop. In these days of proliferating undergraduate and graduate writing programs in American colleges and universities, there are plenty of writing classes available. Many colleges and universities open some classes to people who aren't regular students. Others have special extension programs, offering classes at night or on weekends. Community colleges offer classes. Often they are taught by people who are writers themselves, and they offer the opportunity for active and detailed group discussion at an essentially professional level.

c. The graduate writing program. This involves a big investment of time and money, and all-out commitment. You're going to give up a year or two of your life in exchange for classroom experience, advice from professionals and the benefit of workshop discussion of your fiction.

Another option is the summer writers' conference. With the exception of the workshop at Bennington and the Clarion Writers Conference, most of those available offer courses for no more than two weeks at most, which means they are not as useful as long-term arrangements in helping you locate regular readers.

In all these situations, you make friends outside group meetings, including, perhaps, the one who becomes your trusted first reader. Most people in discussion groups and workshops exchange work on an informal basis outside group meetings, with writers zeroing in on the others in the group who are most in tune with what they are doing.

3. *Hit the Front Line.* You have to be feeling fairly strong to do this, because we're talking about sending your manuscript to somebody who's going to judge it as fit or unfit for publication. Your story or novel has to be in good enough shape to withstand professional scrutiny, and you personally have to be feeling strong enough to live with rejection.

There is, however, an interim position. You may want to get your feet wet by sending a covering letter and a brief sample of your work to a literary agent in hopes that you'll find somebody willing to represent you. Naturally, your letter should be as compelling as possible, and you're going to stand a better chance if you've managed to garner a couple of publications.

Assuming you're at Square One, that brings you to the bottom line, which is also the front line. You're going to have to try to get published.

This means mailing your manuscript to an editor or publisher who you think may like it. The risks are clear:

a. The rejection slip. Once it comes, at least you know not everybody loves your manuscript. By now you've achieved some distance from your story — the weeks or months it takes the professional reader to make a decision. If your story comes back, don't send it right back out automatically. Sit down and reread it. If it still looks as good to you as it did the first time you mailed it, then by all means try two or three more submissions. If the rejection has identified story problems for you, *go back to the drawing board.*

b. The qualified rejection. This is the letter or rejection slip that says no, and then explains why. In spite of what you might think, most writers take the qualified rejection as a good sign. It means the editor or publisher was interested enough in the manuscript to take the time to dignify it — and the writer — with a personal comment. Editors don't write these notes just to be nice. They write them because they've seen something in your work that interests them. If they respond with details about what you might do to make this story better, you have your blueprint for revision. Rewrite and resubmit. You just may be in business.

Clearly, there are many ways of testing your work. If you've put a story or a novel through one or more of them and you still get negative signals, then it's time to reconsider. It still needs work.

## WHAT'S NEXT?

Let's say you've taken one or more or all of these steps, and although people may like certain things about what you've written, they don't like the work as a whole. It becomes clear that there's still a gap between what you thought you were doing and what you've actually accomplished.

This means in spite of what you told yourself when you wrote "the end" at the bottom of your piece and said, "there" and handed it to other readers or mailed it, *you're not finished.* Your piece isn't doing what you wanted it to.

Ask yourself:

1. Are these readers right?
2. If so, do I know what the problem really is?
3. Do I know what to do about it?

If the answers to all three of these questions are yes, then you're ready to go ahead with your revision.

If the answers are no, particularly if you're a beginning writer, you've reached a delicate point in which you have to decide whether to push forward with this piece or whether it's time to cut your losses.

### *Triage*

Hard-pressed medics in the old days went among the wounded on the battlefield, practicing something called *triage.* This meant looking into the faces of each of the wounded and deciding which ones were going to profit most from medical attention. Since the medics were short-staffed, they couldn't waste time working on patients who were going to die anyway.

1. If consistent negative readings and a number of rejections have shaken your faith in a piece of work, then it's probably time to cut your losses. This doesn't mean throwing it out. It means putting it away. In the time you spend working on something new, work that's put aside will either get stronger in your imagination or it will die quietly. Either way, you win. You've achieved the necessary distance and you've done something even more important; by refusing to waste time mourning, you've feathered your nest with a new piece of fiction.

2. If consistent negative readings and rejections give you a clear set of signals that point the way to a successful revision, you've gained ground. It's time to take in the wounded piece of fiction and get your priorities in order.

There's more work to be done.

But let's backtrack. The question posed by this chapter was how to find out whether you're finished when you think you're finished. You let your work fly and saw it shot down like a wild duck on its way to a happier place.

Naturally you don't want that to happen to this story again, or to the next one or the next one. As you revise this time, as you begin the next story or the next, *protect yourself*.

When you send this piece out again, you want it to be as strong as you can make it. This means asking yourself a series of hard questions about style, character and truth of dialogue, story and setting. It means standing back from the whole and considering a structural revision.

I've suggested that wide reading is going to give you a good basis for comparison, a sense of form and a more highly developed power of judgment. It's also going to help point the way to more effective writing.

Add to this background of reading a list of questions you should ask yourself, *as you're writing* and *as you're revising*.

Part of the business of this book is to provide some of these questions. I want to help you shortstop criticism and arm yourself against rejection by making a habit of asking yourself all the hard questions I'm going to pose in coming chapters.

These hard questions are designed to engage you in the process of total revision. Forewarned is forearmed. Once you make them part of your working equipment, you'll be able to make revision a way of life.

Because your house of words is precisely that—something you are making out of words—you'll want to work with the best available materials.

Because this means making the words march *in the right direction so your story will move in the right direction*, we'll begin by talking about style.

From the first page you write, you're making countless narrative decisions—from establishing point of view to naming and placement of characters in time and physical location to the nature of characters' relationships. Because what you as storyteller say is, essentially, *inseparable from the way in which you say it*, we're going to start by discussing style and numbering the kinds of questions you ought to be asking yourself as you write.

## CHAPTER 5

# BUILDING YOUR STORY

STORIES ARE MADE OUT OF WORDS.

The idea for a story may come before the words do, but if you want to get your idea across to readers, you have to use words to do it. If you're going to be a storyteller and not a filmmaker or a draftsman or a master painter, then words are your materials. You'll want to work with the best ones.

When you're making a house of words, you have to pay particular attention to your opening. *From the beginning* the way you write is important, because the words you choose to open your story are going to invite the reader to pick your story up — or put it down. What's more, the opening paragraphs set the tone and make the rules for that particular story. As author, you're beginning to make choices. With every sentence you write, you're making narrative decisions. Making choices, you're establishing your style.

Now let's look at some of the things style does for you.

## YOUR STYLE SETS UP YOUR STORY

The way you write helps define and determine what you're writing. Choosing words to begin a story, you're establishing the ground rules — how you're going to deal with your material.

Say you begin by describing a night. It is an August night in Washington, D.C.: hot, close, noisy, empty of people and crowded with memories. The waters of three A.M. are closing over your character's head: the dark night of the soul from which there is no emerging.

Notice that although we have only four lines here, and this is only a summary, *something is happening*. Each adjective defines and qualifies. Every choice creates something: time, place, mood, situation. Now let's pretend I've decided to make something of these elements.

> Martin had spent too many Augusts in Washington; the streets were filled with wraiths of former selves—happy people who could not hear his warnings. Even though it was so hot that nobody was out and nothing moved, he could almost see the two of them drifting down Independence Avenue—Martin and beautiful, lost Carla walking through shimmering heat mirages. He wanted to reach out and touch the lovers, to beg them to stop and reconsider, but in the next second they were gone and he was adrift again, cut loose in the miasma of three o'clock in the morning.

Enough. In a few lines we know who and where Martin is, that he's trying to outrun an unhappy love story, and that the general tone is going to be both romantic and elegiac. The rhythm sets the mood. Although the time is the present, it's clear that Martin is going to have to come to terms with his past in order to resolve the story. It would appear that the romance was doomed because they made a choice that Martin regrets.

Since this is an example and not the beginning of a story, it has no life beyond this page, but if you or I decided to rewrite it and make a few more decisions, it could turn into something.

This as much as anything explains why I put style and openings together. By choosing words, you are making story. Your prose rhythms become the rhythms of the story. Your word choices become narrative decisions. The words begin working for you. The way you put them together creates your style which in turn defines and distinguishes your story.

Whether you're writing a romance or a mystery or deep psychological fiction, the opening of your story is going to:

1. Identify characters.
2. Determine time and place.
3. Establish point of view.
4. Signal readers as to what kind of story they're reading.

## STYLE KEEPS YOUR STORY ON THE TRACK

Good choices put your story on the right track. The English language is one of the richest and most complicated forms of human expression and the possibilities for inventiveness and power are unlimited. So is the margin for error.

Does a character scurry or scuttle or scramble or slouch? Are the speeches abrupt or flowery? Are the prose rhythms jerky or rambling or smooth? Are your adjectives arcane or colorful or of the garden variety, and while we're at it, are they sparse or plentiful? *Each choice you make is going to make a difference.*

Because it's much easier to do things right the first time than to spend hours undoing wrong choices, do your best to *be precise and be specific.* If you try your best to make the right choices for a particular story from the beginning, it will save you work later. You want to choose the words that will tell your reader *exactly what you mean.* Finding the right words, you'll make sound narrative choices.

### Making Your Story Different from All Other Stories

Someone once said there were only seven stories in the world. Whether there are only seven basic stories or seven hundred thousand makes no difference.

What's important is that there are as many different ways of telling stories as there are people to tell them. When you're working hard and working well, you'll discover that the particular cadences and vocabulary you bring to a story make it yours and no one else's. You want to be able to tell yourself, This story is different from all other stories *because I wrote it.*

When everything in a story or a novel is working right, style and substance are essentially one thing. Readers may be able to identify the style, but they aren't going to be able to separate it from what's going on. Once you've written enough fiction, you'll begin to feel this for yourself and you can see it working in your own stories.

## STYLE TELLS THE READER WHAT TO THINK

A writer friend was watching TV with us. I switched to a channel that gave me a movie sequence of a country cabin, a door opening, a teenager heading up the stairs to spooky music copied from the score Bernard Herrmann wrote for *Psycho*: violin scrape-scrape-scrape/screech-screech-screech. I said, "Oh, horror movie." We watched for a while and it turned out to be *Friday the Thirteenth: Part III*. After a pause, my friend asked, "How did you know it was going to be a horror movie?" How could I NOT know?

Style told me what to expect.

In the same way, prose style can tell your reader what to expect from a story. Prose style gives signals in some of the same ways a movie presents itself. It simultaneously makes the thing what it is and prepares the reader for what's coming.

One kind of prose suggests romance, another suggests the hard-boiled detective story, another the nostalgic first-person narration that signals a story of remembered childhood, or coming of age. The words you choose and the way you put them together let your readers know what kind of story they're reading, whether it's going to be a mystery or a psychological exploration or speculative fiction or gritty, hard-edged urban realism.

It can set and maintain mood, whether it's comic or romantic or taut with suspense or fraught with terror.

When you get really good at what you're doing, you're going to be able to use words to make readers feel what you want them to feel and think what you want them to think. You can use crisp prose to make them race along to find out what's going to happen next or you can slow them down with complex sentences rich with detail.

## WHERE STYLE COMES FROM

I think style is not so much developed as discovered. We all have our own thought patterns and when we talk, our own ways of expressing ourselves. But something happens when we start putting things down on paper: fits of self-consciousness and imitation. It takes a while for most of us to work through all the stages of learning to develop a style of our own.

You can learn about style *from the outside* by reading. You can learn about style *from the inside* by writing. You have to write and write and do more writing in order to find out the best way *for you* to say what you think you want to say.

1. Reading helps you develop an idea of what's good because reading shows you how established writers do things. You find out what succeeds and what doesn't, what you like and what you don't like. Try to figure out how writers you admire use words—whether in excessive sweeps of rhetoric or in tight, simple sentences. You won't want to imitate them, but you will want to know how they manage to do what they're doing.

2. If you read enough different kinds of writers, you begin to get an idea of what style is. You'll discover that there are as many possibilities as there are writers, from the terse prose of Ernest Hemingway to the spare present tense of Jay McInerney and Bret Easton Ellis to F. Scott Fitzgerald's almost romantic treatment of the language to William Faulkner's long, complicated, powerful sentences. You need to read so many different writers that *you don't imitate any of them.*

3. You can learn through listening. When you begin concentrating on dialogue, you'll want to listen to the way other people talk. Right now, try listening to yourself. When you're writing or thinking about writing, or simply thinking about something that's just happened, what are your rhythms? What does your prose sound like? Chances are it doesn't sound the same way it does when you've just finished reading somebody

else's work. You're likely to walk away from a novel by Henry James or Raymond Chandler or Samuel R. Delany framing sentences like James or Chandler or Delany, but if you're patient, the symptoms will pass. You're listening for your own prose rhythms. Eventually you're going to find them.

4. Try to get it down on paper—the way *you personally* describe things. You're going to find your style through writing, writing and more writing. This is where the real work comes in. Sitting down to write the first time, or even at the end of the first year or the second one, you're not alone. You're probably hearing echoes of the last thing you read. In the old days beginning writers sounded like Faulkner or Hemingway; now they're likely to sound more like Bret Easton Ellis, a beginning writer himself. You have to work past this stage, and the best way is by reading widely as you write more and more. If you read enough, you'll read so much that you won't be able to remember it all. If you keep writing, sooner or later you're going to break through all the borrowed styles and hit your stride. It's not easy, but it pays off.

5. You can learn through revision. Revising a first, second or fifth draft, you'll sharpen and determine *what you are doing* by paying attention to *the way you're doing it*. This will help you:

1. See the work as a whole.
2. Complete your thinking.
3. Bring your story to satisfactory completion.

In the next chapter, we'll move on into specific questions you can ask yourself about the opening of your story—and the way you tell it.

## CHAPTER 6

---

# THINKING LIKE A WRITER

How do you move from a first draft to a finished story?

Try to stop being a writer for the moment, and become a reader. Sit down and read your story. Now ask yourself:

1. Is my story doing what I want it to do?
2. If not, why not?
3. Have I said *exactly what I mean*?
4. What can I do to make my story do what I want it to?

You are already thinking about revision.

Now it's time to reread that story. This time, you're going to think like a writer.

Remember, revision should be part of the process of composition. If you learn to revise willingly, you're going to become so familiar with the process that in time you will start making some of these decisions *as you compose.*

The questions you ask yourself after reading a first draft or a tenth one are the same questions you ought to be asking yourself from the minute you sit down to write. Ask them AS YOU GO. The better you answer them, the surer your touch is going to be as your story unfolds.

Once you get in the habit, revision is going to become part of your working equipment.

## WHERE TO BEGIN

Even as there's no right or wrong way to compose, there's no single right way to go about revision. There's no right or wrong order in which to ask yourself specific questions about revision. In an ideal world, you'd be able to think about all questions *all at once* — as you write and as you revise.

Because most of us find it difficult to do this, we need to sort out the elements of fiction so we can stand off and take a good look at our work. The detailed series of checklists that follow will give you an opportunity to take apart and analyze the different elements of fiction and will provide you with a series of questions to ask about your work.

Writers may differ on where to begin but everybody agrees that you've got to start somewhere. Although some writers prefer to try to separate style and substance, saying that they're reading first for story or shape or organization or whatever, and will fix up the prose later, it's clear that at some level they, too, are reading to find out how well the words they've chosen do the job.

Since I believe strongly in the organizational power of words, I'm going to make the checklist on style the first of our series of checklists designed to help you read for revision.

Since word choices create beginnings and establish narrative ground rules, you'll find it useful to read for revision to find out *how well the words are telling the story.* As you're using words to tell the reader what to think, you'll want to be sure they're working for you.

Remember, *by getting the words in order, you're getting your thoughts in order.*

I'm not talking about proofreading. Making the right words march in the right direction, you are controlling and shaping your story. Style isn't cosmetic. It's not like paint, that you put on a house after it's finished so it will look nice. It is the fabric.

Reading with attention to the way the words are telling the story, you're also:

1.  Getting a sense of organization — whether events are in the right order.

2.  Getting a sense of shape — whether your story is all there or whether there's something missing.

3. Completing your thinking. If passages are unclear to you, they're going to be unclear to your reader. *You are figuring out what you have to say as you work on the way you're saying it.*

4. Reading for consistency of style and tone and character and story.

Judging how well your writing does the job, you can ask yourself several questions. Answering them, you're on your way to sounding like yourself and nobody else.

## CHECKLIST I: QUESTIONS ABOUT STYLE

1. *Am I saying what I mean?* If math is one of the two major systems of logic, language is the other. Put your prose in good working order and you'll get your thoughts in order.

When you sat down to write you may have been fired by inspiration, but every one of your sentences had better parse — subject, predicate, clauses all in order and all in the right place. This is easy to do with simple, unadorned prose. If you're just beginning it might be wise to keep it simple until you've learned control. Once you have control of your prose, you can do anything you want with it. You can build elaborate constructions. You can grab a sentence by the tail and swing it around your head.

If you don't have a grammar manual, get one. The old classics are Fowler's *Modern English Usage* and *The Elements of Style* by Strunk and White, but most publishers now offer up-to-date and easy-to-read references. You should have one at hand when you're composing and again when you're rewriting. The rule?

*When in doubt, look it up.*

Bad grammar can further confuse your thinking and shoot down your story before it ever gets off the ground.

2. *Are my word choices working for or against me?*
   a. Can I find a fresher way to say what I want to say? If you can't think of a new way to say what you have to say, you may not have anything new to tell the reader. Working hard to avoid cliché, you are going to sharpen your thinking. Wide reading is going to enrich your vocabulary and a little

thought will help you choose words that say precisely what you mean.

b. Am I overloading my text with too many adjectives, distracting readers with bizarre word choices or trying to force words into new meanings?

c. Am I using this word right? If you're working with an unfamiliar word—OK, let's say, something as exotic as *etiolated*, or *querulous*—you'd better be sure you're using it right. Again,
*When in doubt, look it up.*

d. Do I have the right word in the first place? This is the question you need to ask yourself now, as you begin revising, and at every stage of composition. Part of the process of finding out what you have to say is choosing the right words to express it. Is it spelled right? At best, misspellings alienate editors and make you look like an amateur. At worst, misspellings change meanings—guerilla/gorilla, complaisant/complacent—and things as simple as hear/here and their/there are examples that come immediately to mind. They get between you and what you have to say.

Another rule: *Precision creates and emphasizes meaning*.

e. Can I be more specific? If you have a character getting into her car, is she getting into a '79 Datsun or an '89 Mercedes or what? Is it hers or is it stolen? Specifics advance your story. If somebody is being assailed by an armed mugger, what is he carrying—a knife, a gun or a banana wrapped in a handkerchief? It's going to determine how both characters behave.

3. *What about sentence variety?* There's no immediate rule of thumb here, but if you have a story in which every sentence starts with *he*, you may need to wake up your reader.

4. *Are my sentences run-on?* Teachers fight like tigers to get students to break up overloaded sentences because they know that they can obscure meaning and exhaust the reader. Some writers think fiction lowers all the barriers and that rambling can create velocity. Think again. Go back and make certain that, long or short, all those sentences are perfectly clear.

5. *Do I need to break up paragraphs?* If a paragraph runs for more than half a page, you're going to need to subject it to close

scrutiny. Ideas get lost in overblown paragraphs. So do readers.

6. *What about mannerisms?* Omitting articles isn't style. Neither is putting a period between each word of a sentence and neither is coining words the way some poets do (made up words like wave-shifting and feather-troubled are not effective adjectives). Strange typographical setup isn't style and neither are sentence fragments.

7. *Do I sound like me, or like the last writer I read?* If there's something *faintly familiar* about the way your story tells itself, try to step back and see whose work it looks like. Whether consciously or unconsciously, most beginning writers imitate. If you've written a William Faulkner story—or even one by the new literary brat pack—you're going to want to try to find a more individual way of expressing yourself.

8. *Do I need to make word or phrase cuts to make my prose more effective?* Look at these two versions of one sentence:

After he got up and got dressed that morning sleepy Harry went slowly down to the corner store, where he walked inside and found Mr. Bissell being held up by an armed robber.

Set this against the more specific:

Sleepy Harry shambled into the corner store, where he found Mr. Bissell being held at gunpoint by an armed robber.

# BEGINNINGS

This last example brings us neatly to the next matter. It's clear that by making cuts in the Harry sentence in the last of the style questions, I was doing two things:

1. I was sharpening a sentence to make it more effective.

In the process, I was taking the most direct route to the action.

2. Reaching for more expressive words, I was writing an opening.

When you've read widely enough you'll be able to see for yourself that when fiction is working, style and content become the same thing. Refining word choices and forging the logic of the sentences, you're completing your thinking and developing your story. Even the rough example above shows how this works. Refining those few words, I was making several narrative decisions.

It's clear in one sentence that the Harry/armed robber story is being told in the third person, but from Harry's point of view. That means Harry is the camera. It also begins more or less in the middle of the action, with a Harry/armed robber confrontation. Moving through a few more sentences with Harry, I'd know better who he was by how he *reacted* to this situation — familiar store-owner (remember, Harry knows his name) at gunpoint, and so early in the morning!

Because I am a confessed block constructer — rewriting sentence by sentence before I move on — I believe that the opening casts the style at the same time the style casts the opening. As I suggested in Chapter Five, it's these opening sentences that invite or discourage readers. You want to give them your best. As you do, important things are happening to your story.

Let's look at the openings of three novels, beginning with F. Scott Fitzgerald's *The Great Gatsby*:

> In my younger and more vulnerable years my father gave me some advice that I've been turning over in my mind ever since.
>
> "Whenever you feel like criticizing anyone," he told me, "just remember that all the people in this world haven't had the advantages that you've had."

In these two short paragraphs we're introduced to the narrator, who clearly is a member of what used to be called the upper classes. He's going to tell us this story, and although we don't yet know what the story's going to be, we know him pretty well through his speech rhythms. The author has, furthermore, established that this is going to be a first-person story and because the narrator is talking about judging people, and his tone is just a little distant, it's fairly clear that although he's involved in what's going on, he's not at the center of the action. What's more, he's talking about the past.

Fitzgerald has grabbed you by the lapels and told you how to listen to what his narrator has to say—reserving judgment. He's also setting the tone for what is to follow.

Now listen to this first-person narrator.

> If you really want to hear about it, the first thing you'll probably want to know is where I was born, and what my lousy childhood was like, and how my parents were occupied and all before they had me, and all that David Copperfield kind of crap, but I don't feel like going into it, if you want to know the truth. In the first place, that stuff bores me, and in the second place, my parents would have about two hemorrhages apiece if I told anything pretty personal about them . . .

That's J. D. Salinger's Holden Caulfield; again, the narrator has gotten your attention and he's pulling you into *Catcher in the Rye*. These much-imitated rhythms let us know the narrator is a rebel, and he's young.

In both cases, the authors have used first-person narrators to gain our confidence and involve us in what's going on.

Using the third person present tense, Bobbie Ann Mason begins *In Country* this way:

> "I have to stop again, hon," Sam's grandmother says, tapping her on the shoulder. Sam Hughes is driving, with her uncle, Emmett Smith, half asleep beside her.
> "Where are we?" grunts Emmett.
> "Still on I-64. Mawmaw has to go to the restroom."
> "I forgot to take my pill when we stopped last," Mawmaw says.

In a few short lines of dialogue, Mason has pulled us right into the middle of a scene and introduced her principal characters. She has set the narrative tone and established the style.

In these three cases I think manner and matter are inseparable, as they are in all successful fiction.

This means the careful writer is going to give extra time and thought to the opening pages of any short story or novel, revising sentence by sentence, draft by draft, going back after the last draft to read once more for style and appropriateness of the opening.

One good way to develop an ear for good openings is to go back and read the first paragraphs of every story in an anthology, or to pick up a bunch of novels at random and look at the first few lines. You're going to know soon enough which ones take hold of your imagination on first sight and pull you in.

I've already listed a number of questions you can ask yourself about style. As you look at your story, add to them these questions about your opening.

## CHECKLIST II: QUESTIONS ABOUT YOUR OPENING

1. *Does my story really begin here?* Too many beginning writers have to talk their way into a story, describing settings and characters to themselves at great length before they can get them moving. Now it's time to go back and *get rid of everything you wrote in order to find out what you were writing*.

2. *Is my opening too long for what it does?* There are many areas of risk here:

a. The lengthy description narrowing in on a house, a room, a person — the fictional equivalent of the movies' slow zoom in. It works better in pictures.

b. Several minutes of people talking in which nothing happens.

c. Several minutes of your character getting up in the morning.

Check your openings on a case-by-case basis. You're going

to need the whole story in front of you before you can be really sure.

3. *Is my opening too long in proportion to the rest of the story?* Because the first scene is usually on paper before anything else, some writers may be inclined to keep reworking until it's over-developed—an overelaborate setup for something that should be neat and swift.

4. *Is my opening interesting?* Is there a narrative hook—some incident, some question posed here that will catch the reader's interest? Is anybody else going to like this as well as I do or is an outsider going to think it's boring? Keeping this question in mind, ask yourself the next one.

5. *What about action?* Is there something going on? Are my characters immediately engaged in a clash of wills or brought face to face with an impending problem or surprise or confrontation? Openings should imply coming action and interaction.

6. *Is my opening clear?* Is my reader going to know who these people are, who's talking, what's happening? Can my reader tell what's going on? A touch of mystery never hurt anything, but the reader who is left at sea in the middle of unexplained happenings may not stay around long enough to have them explained.

7. *Have I chosen a flashy opening at the expense of continuity?* Often beginning writers will start with the right instincts—finding themselves engaged with character in mid-scene, only to have to go back to explain everything in an attack of what I call the *had-hads*: "It *had* been ten years since Mary and Todd *had* gotten divorced and Todd's new wife Reba *had* . . ." You can avoid this by starting at the beginning—or assuming your story starts here and filling in background by implication (phrases like "since the divorce" or: "in this postwar society" give the reader the idea and you, as writer, *take the past for granted* instead of feeling compelled to explain) or by well-handled flashbacks, if they don't get in the way.

Other beginning writers start with a bang and then find that they've left themselves with *too much to explain*. Trying to cover their tracks by accounting for everything, they're likely to slow down action and distract the reader with a muddy time scheme — too many flashbacks and, worse yet, flashbacks within flashbacks. A good exercise for a story that has developed time problems is to identify and number events *chronologically* and then do your best to reduce the number of time shifts.

Still others begin with a prologue set in the deep past and then leap forward to time present without ever intending to return to the past. Since readers remember best *the first thing you tell them*, be sure you want this moment from the past to be central to the story. See if you can make it work without the initial flashback.

8. *Now that I know how my story comes out, is this the right opening*? Sometimes, this is a matter of tone. You thought this was going to be a serious story but early on it became a funny one. Now go back and rewrite so the parts of your story match.

At other times, rereading a finished draft with the benefit of hindsight, writers discover that there are things they know now that they didn't know when they began. There may be details they can add to the opening they have, or they may find out the story doesn't begin quite where they thought it did. This may mean adding a new scene — or getting rid of one.

9. *If I've written a wonderful opening, does the rest of my story measure up to it*? This means making sure you've maintained the level of energy and excitement you started with. It may mean rewriting the rest until it is as good as your opening.

10. *Are all the shotguns I planted in the first scene fired by the end of the story*? Sometimes we throw in details in the heat of invention — a long-lost sister or an undiscovered secret or a family battle going on somewhere offstage — and then lose track of them. *Everything in a story has to function in terms of the story*. If that long-lost sister or undiscovered secret or family battle doesn't turn out to be relevant to your finished story, *take it out*.

## REVISION AS ORGANIC WHOLE

Notice that although I chose to begin the checklists with considerations of style and opening, these are really questions about the work as a whole, as are all considerations of revision.

By the time you've asked yourself question five—Is there something going on?—you've moved past reading for style and effectiveness of opening, and into looking at your story as a whole.

Everything you do to a story affects the story as a whole. This is because living, breathing stories are not assembled out of spare parts stuck on like the moustache on Mr. Potato Head.

Stories are whole.

Moving on from reading for possible revision of style and opening, we can identify the rest of the areas we need to look at to see whether we need to do revising. They are:

- Character
- Dialogue
- Point of view
- Showing versus telling
- Story and structure.

We can even look at them one by one, *as long as we understand that they too are part of a whole.* Revision is an organic process, and although we can look at areas that need revision and talk about ways of revising, we need to understand this. Choosing, cutting, reorganizing—however we revise, we're engaged in a single process.

There's more.

These various ways of looking at and carrying out revision are part and parcel of writing. These questions need to be considered every time you sit down to write. It should be clear as well that although for your convenience I've divided the possibilities for revision under separate headings according to aspects of fiction writing, and am providing separate checklists, every question you ask yourself about revision and every individual step is part of this organic process. At every step along the way, you are:

WRITING FICTION.

## CHAPTER 7

# READING FOR REVISION: CHARACTER, DETAIL

LIKE EVERYTHING YOU WRITE, characters are made out of words. The words you choose create and breathe life into fictional people.

The writer working with character has to create an entire person different from all other people—somebody readers are going to like or dislike according to the writer's intentions, somebody readers can believe in and care about.

Judging our fictional characters, we're going to start with the checklist.

## CHECKLIST III: QUESTIONS ABOUT CHARACTER

1. *Is my character complete?* Although I don't have to put his entire life history down on the page and I don't want to bore readers with explanatory accounts of his emotional state, do I have enough detail here to make a whole person?

2. *Is my character believable?* We can believe in the hopes and fears of college students and early cliff-dwellers and extraterrestrials with neon spines *as long as the psychology is working*. This means examining your character's motives and actions. You may not need to explain why your characters behave in a certain way, but if you want readers to believe in them, you have to understand and believe in the state of mind that brought these people to this moment.

72

3. *Is my character consistent?* Would this character, as drawn, do what I asked him or her to do? Again, even a loving mother can become a hatchet murderer *if the psychology is working.*

4. *Is my character distinctive?* Another way to ask this question is, are there ways in which this character is different from all other characters? Unless you're writing experimental fiction, it's more or less understood that the people you introduce to your readers should have something that distinguishes them — something they do or say or wear or care about that gives the reader a reason to follow their adventures.

5. *Does this character function in this story?* Even the tightest short stories may have a cast of more than a dozen. All of us, however, get caught up in the idea of the occasional colorful character — somebody our protagonist runs into on the way to the real action of the story. If these colorful characters are going to be anything more than extra faces in a crowd, they need to justify their existence.

For example, if your hero has a conversation with a bum on the sidewalk and then goes on to the store and we never hear anything more about the bum and nothing the bum says has anything to do with the story or the outcome, you'd better move that bum out of the story. If on the other hand your hero has a conversation with a bum on the sidewalk and it changes his mood or his mind or his course of action or his way of looking at things, that's another matter.

In short, your secondary characters have to justify the space they take up in your story.

6. *Is this character a stereotype?* Another way to ask this question is, does my character look more like a comic-strip character than a living person?

Some of the broader stereotypes include the prostitute with the heart of gold, the possessive mother, the weedy-looking guy with outrageous daydreams, the misunderstood teenager. This is a list to which you can add some of the stronger characters in the fiction you read. Because we get committed to our characters, this is a hard question to answer honestly. Try.

If your character seems stereotypical or two-dimensional,

ask yourself: Is there some way in which this prostitute/day-dreamer/possessive mother is different from all others? If there is, go back to your story and be sure your reader sees what you see — the quirks and yearnings that make this an individual.

## GETTING INTO CHARACTER

I start with character because I believe characters move together to make story. As there are hundreds of thousands of individual human characteristics, there are hundreds of thousands of indicators of character. They are too many and varied to list, but you can work your way through to an understanding of character by looking at what you've written in the light of your answers to Checklist III.

Talking about what characters *aren't* is sometimes the most direct route into finding out what characters *are*.

If you've reread your story and answered no to most of the questions about your central character, it's time to rethink.

Remember, *character is built from the inside*. Like a method actor, you need to be able to get inside your character's head. For the purposes of the story, you need to be able to see the world as your character sees it and talk and act as your character would.

Let's look at your story again.

## COMPLETENESS

We're going to begin with problems of completeness. If your character is more than a one-dimensional comic-strip stereotype, you're also working with problems of believability, consistency and originality from the moment you start this person moving on the page. Notice I say person.

You're not building an artificial person out of spare parts, which means all the considerations raised in the checklist should be dealt with more or less at the same time.

Because I don't have your story in front of me, I'm going

to run through the checklist with an example of my own. Let's say it begins this way:

The girl hated her mother.

For our purposes, we'll say I have a fairly sensitive story about a young woman who is having a terrible time with her mother. Let's also say I don't have a very good grasp on who this person is *until I begin to complete her.*

You don't need to write an entire fictional autobiography or even a one-page monologue to turn your character into a whole person. You can understand your character better and make the person complete and believable by:

1. Naming. Names are people. Your Alistair and your Aloysius are not the same as Bob or Barry or Zorg, for that matter; your Celeste and Tiffany are not the same as Jane or Mary or Martha or Sylvia, and they aren't going to behave the same way in a story. Add the last name and you get national and ethnic overtones as soon as you move away from the nonspecific Evans or Jones to O'Malley or Chiappa or Wu or Cohen or Washington or Stuchinksi.

While you were out, I named my character Marilyn Zorn. I named her Marilyn because I realize now she's not a girl at all, she's an older woman—thirty-seven, and as I write I understand that the reason she still acts and thinks like a girl is because she is under her mother's thumb. This mother named her Marilyn expecting this would make her beautiful. Our Marilyn isn't. The last name? It expresses the way she feels about things—forlorn.

2. Listen. Characters reveal themselves through dialogue—and thought patterns. The character who says, "Ain't no use even thinking about it" is a different sort of person from the one who says, "Me? Think about that? Are you kidding?" Every time a character speaks or thinks he or she is helping you make narrative decisions.

"Mama, if you would leave me alone for a minute, I'd be able to figure this out—what to do about it." That's Marilyn, and I understand that she's a simple working girl who hates the fact that she's thirty-seven years old and still living with her mother.

3. Put your character into action. What would my imaginary person do when confronted with that robber Harry ran

into in the last chapter? If she picks up a window pole and knocks him out, you have one kind of person. If she goes home and goes to bed and considers the fragility of human arrangements and the relative lack of safety in the urban world, you have another.

But Marilyn isn't even thinking of going to the store. She has other things on her mind. Fixing her mother's pillows, setting up her lunch tray and aiming her at the TV, she is preparing to escape to the office. The "it" she's worrying about in her speech above turns out to be the fact that a man from the office wants to come home to her apartment for dinner. The mother appears to have been badgering Marilyn to invite him and now she's full of suggestions about what Marilyn should wear and what she might do to herself to make herself better-looking.

    a. The jerky, agitated pace at which Marilyn does these chores will indicate her state of mind.

    b. As her mother begins giving beauty tips, Marilyn becomes brisker. There is something final about the way she goes about these tasks she performs every morning that indicates she's at the end of her rope.

    4. Ask yourself: What does this character want? What is this character afraid of?

What Marilyn wants is to be left alone in a world without her mother. She would, in fact, like to be left alone with this man who's coming to dinner. Marilyn would like her mother to shut up and disappear for the evening because *this is what Marilyn is afraid of*: she is afraid that her mother, a chronic invalid who may or may not be really sick, will use her fragile good looks and womanly wiles to steal the potential boyfriend away from her.

    5. Put this character into confrontation. Back to the robber — or to the mate who wants a divorce, or the mother who accuses our character of never phoning and never coming to visit. How does this person behave?

In this case, Marilyn has put the room in order and set up the trays, and is preparing to make her escape when she says, "I'm not bringing him home, Mama. I've put some extra graham crackers and some Cheez Whiz on the tray because I'm getting Bradley to take me out to dinner."

To which her mother says, "Argh," clutches her throat and falls over in a real or perhaps a pretend seizure.

Which is it? What will Marilyn do?

Stay tuned. We aren't talking about story here, we're talking about character.

But you will notice that poor Marilyn, who didn't exist fifteen minutes ago, has begun moving around in her story. We will leave her at her moment of confrontation and hope I've made you care a little bit about the outcome.

## BELIEVABILITY, DISTINCTIVENESS

Let's move on to more detailed ways to address the questions of believability and distinctiveness. If you believe, your readers are going to believe. You are going to believe in your characters *because you're going to become them.*

Begin by hypothesis. Ask yourself, what would I do if I were in this situation I've created for this character? Think it through. Are there differences between you and the character? Say you're a woman writer writing a grandfather. If I were a grandfather I might be more philosophical about what's happening, or angrier; I'm sure my judgment would be affected by rich and complicated memories. About Marilyn. If I were Marilyn I'd prop Mama up in bed, split and call the paramedics from the office, but she's probably a nicer person than I am, and she really cares about this mother in spite of everything. But I'm moving into what comes next.

Continue with imagination. Instead of seeing this character from the outside, try to see the world through his eyes. Start with physical details—his health, how well he's getting around, his eyesight. What about his mood? Is it pessimistic or cheery or what, and do you know why?

Marilyn, as it turns out, is feeling particularly fragile today because she hasn't had a boyfriend in years, she's terrified of being left alone and there are new wrinkles and new sections of dry skin sagging at her throat every time she looks in the mirror. For this woman who still thinks of herself as a girl, every negotiation is hard, every big decision even harder. Shall she leave her mother and go out with Bradley? What will she do if Mama is really sick this time, and may just die on her?

Move into the character so you can move with the character. For the purposes of this revision, you are this character. Later you will become every character you write, seeing all the faces, doing all the voices.

Marilyn flutters between the door and the telephone. She tiptoes back to the bedroom door and sees her mother still lying in that unnatural position, with her beautiful head tossed back and a thin thread of saliva staining the pillow.

Next, move outside so you can see your character. Notice I have left this for last, because I believe that if you're able to *become* your character, you may not need to know what this person looks like because you feel it. But now it's time to see how she looks to you—stature, coloring, clothes, way of moving. As you might guess, our Marilyn is underweight, pale and timid. Unlike her vivid mother, who has just thrown this real or imaginary seizure, she moves slowly and cautiously, as if afraid of disturbing the air in the room around her.

Now ask yourself how she looks to the other characters— attractive or not, bizarre or off-putting or lovable or dangerous. You will see this by moving them into scenes together. Becoming both Marilyn and her mother/Bradley/other people at the office, you'll discover *how she acts when she's with other people*. There is always a gap between self-image and the way others see us. Until they meet other people, our characters often think like—well, *ourselves*. Encounters make fictional characters three-dimensional.

Although Marilyn sees herself the way I do, she is attractive to Bradley, at the office, because she has good features and the delicately drawn romantic look of some tuberculosis victims. To her mother, who I know now is only pretending to be unconscious, she looks awkward and funny and juvenile and stupid.

This moment of crisis is going to prove to Marilyn—and us—*who she really is*.

Now that you've seen your character from the outside, notice how the other characters treat him or her and how this character responds to others in the story. By this time, you've moved far beyond consideration of character into matters of story — but you probably also understand that you moved into story the minute you got inside this character.

I know I did. If I stick with Marilyn for a few more minutes I'm going to have to put this chapter aside and write her story.

By the time you've done all these things for your imaginary person, your character has become real to you — speech patterns established, everything from costume and likes and dislikes to loves and hates seems to follow naturally. You already know what this person is going to do in a given situation. But you need to know how to make the reader see and hear what you see and hear, to set this character apart.

## Distinctiveness

You can use physical detail to make your character's differences apparent. If a character is wearing trousers, are they jeans or baggies or gray flannels or tennis whites or what? If they are jeans and the character is a woman, are they Levis or Gloria Vanderbilts? It makes a difference. If your woman character is a compulsive reader it's going to make some difference to let us know whether she's hooked on SF or Barbara Cartland or running around with a copy of Kirkegaard.

You can tell us more about this person by describing the room or house or the apartment — whether it's furnished in high tech or threadbare stuff from a second-hand store or ancestral bits and pieces or outmoded Danish modern and you can tell us even more by letting us know what objects this person cherishes — the string bracelet given by an old friend or the religious medal from a teacher or the Mexican sculpture, or . . .

The possibilities are endless.

Let's say that for her day's adventure, which I think now is going to end not at the office but in the Emergency Room (while we weren't looking Marilyn has phoned the paramedics), Marilyn has selected a pretty three-piece knit in a soft beige, something that would look appropriate on a much younger person. Because she has something of the madcap about her, she has added to the rosy pearls with matching clip-on earrings a little girl's barrette, the pink plastic kind in the shape of a bow ribbon. She has it flattening a curl she particularly wants to have look nice when she gets to the office, but I already know she's going to forget to remove it when the time comes for the big confrontation with Bradley.

She and Mama live in a one-bedroom apartment. Marilyn sleeps on a daybed in the living room, and on the walls you will find a tiered shelf with Marilyn's collection of angels, including the Hummel angel that sits on the edge of the shelf and blows a trumpet. Although she doesn't go to church, Marilyn seems to be a somewhat religious person. Let's say she's afraid there is a God with a hell He can send people to, which may be why she called the paramedics.

Deciding on such things, I am dealing with detail. So will you, in making your characters more specific. Each detail shows the reader something specific to that particular character and helps make your character distinctive.

## CONSISTENCY

Because you're working with your character *from the inside*, you've automatically done away with problems of consistency. If you are consistently this character, then this character is going to behave consistently. If your loving mom does indeed do a remarkable about-face and turns into a hatchet murderer, she's going to be a believable hatchet murderer *because the psychology is right*.

By the time you know your character this well, you're going to know what this person is doing in this story and you won't even need to ask yourself how this character responds to other people. Characters imagined *from the inside* justify their presence in the story.

Did you have any doubt Marilyn would call the ambulance and take her mother to the Emergency Room? I didn't.

But the laugh is on Mama. There's nothing the matter with her, but they're going to keep her overnight for tests and further observation. In a truly just world, the doctor would come back to Marilyn and tell her the mother has been fooling her all these years, and for both of their good they should have separate apartments. But because doctors are conservative in their judgments (as are Mama and Marilyn) and are unlikely to suggest radical changes, he'll probably send Mama home with a tranquilizer the very next morning.

But meanwhile Marilyn is going to have one evening of bliss with Bradley, and we can hope this means the beginning of good things for her. Released by her mother's doctor, who has told her to leave this in his hands and get about her business, Marilyn has gone back to the office. Bradley greets her, smiling.

"What about my dinner invitation?"

"Tonight," she says.

He'd always thought she was attractive. What he can't figure out now is why she's smiling quite so broadly.

## TWO KEY QUESTIONS

Now you have to ask yourself whether a given character belongs in a story. The rule of thumb, I think, is that if the character functions in some way—acting and reacting with the central character—if the presence of a given character *affects the outcome*, then that character has justified his or her presence.

The hardest question any of us can put to ourselves about our characters is whether they are stereotypes. Notice how fond I have become of Marilyn in a few short pages. Unfortunately she—and Mama—probably are stereotypes, because I am not delving very deeply into imagination and I'm not drawing on memory at all to make this story.

If they are at all distinctive, it's because I've identified them with specific details—Marilyn's collection of angels, the ailing mother's fading beauty.

I think that if you are working with people you know from the inside and you care enough about them, you can—and should—avoid stereotype. Precision and detail can turn even minor characters into living, breathing people. In spite of the fact that she's a stereotype, the prostitute with the heart of gold turns up again and again in fiction—which succeeds only to the degree that the writer has cared enough about her and her story to turn her into a real person.

The adolescent who is coming of age is another staple character in fiction, but usually the authors avoid stereotype through use of *specific detail*. Because coming-of-age novels are usually semi-autobiographical, authors automatically avoid stereotype because they're using specific, intensely personal details from their own lives. The trick, then, is to bring this kind of specificity to all your characters as you bring them to life.

## DETAIL

You'll do this the same way I brought Marilyn and her mother to the page: through use of detail. Think about the physical details—what your characters look like, what they wear, use, buy, eat; what kinds of rooms they live in; what the streets they walk through look like and what the weather's like.

Then, looking at what you've already written, ask yourself:

1. Have I used enough detail? You want to give readers enough information so they can see what you see—where your character is, and what's happening. Details bring people and scenes to life. Although there's no absolute rule for giving enough detail, you can proceed from the assumption that sentences like: "She had a lot of things in her apartment" and "He put on a hat" sound a little vague. Read authors like John Cheever and John Updike to see what you can make detail do for you.

2. Have I used too much detail? If the detail doesn't enhance the story or advance the action, cut it out. There are no hard and fast rules but I can give some indication of what I'm talking about by saying that if any of your sentences look like this next one, you may be in trouble.

She was wearing her purple silk dress with the brown peplum with the little tucks in it and the matching shoes with
the purple silk stockings that she had bought with Harold
on the first day of their honeymoon which was in Cape Cod
instead of Bermuda because even at the beginning Harold
didn't have any money.

I'd probably get rid of the peplum and the tucks and the first
reference to Harold and come up with something like this:

> She was wearing her purple silk with the matching
> stockings that she'd bought at the Cape, where they'd hon-
> eymooned because even at the beginning Harold didn't
> have any money.

This brings us to questions of cutting, which I'll discuss at length
in later chapters.

3. Can I be more specific? If you've sent your character out
to a restaurant, you're going to tell your readers more about the
character and the situation if you identify it as a fern bar, greasy
spoon, three-star restaurant, chili dog stand or Chinese take-out
place. If your character has bought her lover a watch as a present, we're going to get a clearer idea of what's going on if we
know whether it's a Swatch or a Cartier tank watch.

The idea is not to fill space with further details, but to select
carefully and make the details you do use go to work for you.

4. Do the details I've chosen enhance meaning? This is a
clever question, and one you want to ask only after you've chosen details to set the scene and make your characters specific
and distinctive.

You may be surprised and delighted to discover that some of
your choices have extra significance. If your thwarted lover
sends roses and they arrive dead, you're saying more than something about the roses. You're sending signals that the romance
is in trouble.

If your out-of-work watchsmith picks up a hammer and
starts smashing clocks and watches, he's doing more than indi-

cating rage. He's destroying all those emblems of time passing and at the same time trashing his way of life.

Enough. I think you should choose details because they are the right ones to make the reader see what you see and believe what you believe. Be precise and careful and every detail you choose will add meaning to your work.

Now ask yourself:

1. Are my characters complete and believable?
2. Are they consistent?
3. What makes them different from all other characters?
4. Have I used the right details to bring them to life on the page?
5. Do they sound like real people?

This brings us logically to the next section.

## What's Next

You've probably already noticed that it's impossible for me to talk about any one part of a story without talking about all the other parts. This means that my suggestions for revision to further develop and strengthen character are really ways to make story. As I move on to discuss reading for revision of dialogue, this same thing is going to be true.

I'm talking about dialogue next because dialogue informs character in two ways.

1. Speech patterns determine and define character.
2. We know character through action, and *dialogue is action*.

## CHAPTER 8

# READING FOR REVISION: DIALOGUE IS ACTION

BEFORE YOU CAN ASK YOURSELF whether your dialogue passages are working as well as they should, you need to know what makes good fictional dialogue.

You're going find out where dialogue comes from and develop a sense of what makes good fictional dialogue by paying more careful attention to a couple of things you're already doing.

You need to learn to listen more closely. Most fiction writers walk around with their heads full of voices. These include things heard, remembered and imagined—the raw material for fictional dialogue. These voices come from a number of places— the present, the past and, perhaps more important, from your own imagination.

Unless you are a hermit without TV, telephone or even radio, you hear voices all day every day—voices of friends and family, what comes in over the airwaves, overheard conversation.

Add to the voices you hear coming in every day, the hundreds of recent and past conversations replaying in your memory. As you remember them, you're already editing, cutting and ordering these conversations, omitting nonessential speeches and digressions. You remember not complete conversations, but the *sense* of these conversations.

Now for imagination. If you've begun writing fiction, you probably spend time thinking about your stories even when you aren't actually writing. Most fiction writers hear voices all the time—their characters telling, complaining, remarking. Listen carefully and your characters will tell you who they are, what they want and what they care about. They can even let you know what's going to happen next in your story.

You can learn technique through reading. Reading annual "best" anthologies, contemporary magazines, acknowledged masterpieces and new fiction, you can learn *how other writers create good dialogue.*

A look at a dialogue passage in any story by John O'Hara or Ernest Hemingway, for instance, can teach you a lot about technique. Both of these rather spare writers catch the sound of human speech—notice, I don't say they catch *human speech.* Instead they go through a process of editing and refining that catches the *sound.* They skip the uhms and ahs and repetitions and awkward pauses of actual-time-elapsed conversation between two people to give readers tight duets and trios. These two literary tough guys have much to show us because they strip the process of writing dialogue to the bare bones.

Because Southern writers are particularly attuned to cadences—the "tune" people keep when they say what they have to say—Southern writers like Flannery O'Connor and Eudora Welty have a lot to teach you about natural speech rhythms.

Reading widely, start looking critically at dialogue passages by writers you admire. Ask yourself:

- Is this scene effective and is everything clear? An effective scene moves the characters from point A to point B—from accord to conflict, for instance, or from ignorance to discovery. Successful scenes demonstrate a change in the relationship between the speakers. This is another way of saying that in successful scenes, something *happens.* Try drawing a line through the scene—seeing what the dramatic movement is, who the speakers are, what's at stake. How did the writer manage this?

- Is this dialogue realistic? If so, why? Is this ordinary speech, or is it really ordinary speech that's been edited and intensified for effect?

- If not, why not? Writers like William Faulkner and Joyce Carol Oates are given to writing occasional long, complicated speeches that don't sound like the usual exchanges between ordinary people. What gives these

speeches their power?
- What did this writer put in and leave out to make this scene dramatic? Swift?

# ELEMENTS OF GOOD DIALOGUE

Working on your ear for dialogue—the way you *listen* to voices, and looking at the way other people write good fictional dialogue, you're getting ready to start asking similar questions about your own work. It may help to add a few simple rules.

## *Rule One: Dialogue Is Action*

Except in extreme circumstances, most late 20th-century people don't hit and yell very often. They are, however, capable of acts of enormous power and violence which they carry out through speech.

Every time one of your characters says something to another of your characters and the other says something back, they are *acting* and *reacting*.

This means that every scene you write where people meet and talk should have some movement through it. Dialogue passages should move characters from point A to point B. Your characters can meet and do something as big as falling in love or having a fight or as subtle as shifting from a position of initial wariness to one of trust. They can demonstrate like or dislike, dominance and submission, or deception or betrayal. Anything can happen *as long as something happens* in every dialogue passage you write.

Read for this as you listen to your characters talk. If there is no interaction and no movement, then you need to go back and rewrite.

## *Rule Two: The Most Direct Route to Good Dialogue Is Cutting*

The writer climbs into the head of two or more characters and *listens* to what they have to say to each other, recording everything more or less verbatim. There are certain things we all have to write to find out what we're going to write.

When they get going, fictional characters, like ordinary people, are likely to be long-winded. Even more than people do, fictional characters need to talk and talk in order to find out what they really have to say.

This means the writer has to read and reread dialogue while composing and again while revising, eliminating speeches in which *nothing is happening*. This means getting rid of everything these people said on their way to saying what's important.

Because dialogue is a strangely personal thing, specific to each writer in relationship to each individual piece of fiction, there's no real way to make one or two writers' work stand for all fiction. Although it would be interesting to apply these rules to the work of Faulkner and company, what you really need to know is how they're going to affect what you're doing.

With this in mind, I've constructed a simple example to show you how to make them work. We'll call the following exchange between Harry and Joe our *working example*.

*Harry:* Hi Joe.
*Joe:* Hi, Harry. What's new?
*Harry:* Nothing much.
*Joe:* Nice morning.
*Harry:* If you say so.
*Joe:* Well, it *is* a nice morning, isn't it?
*Harry:* How am I supposed to know if it's a nice morning?
*Joe:* I just thought I would ask. How are you?
*Harry:* Don't ask. How are you?
*Joe:* I'm fine, how are you?
*Harry:* I'm OK, except for the roof.
*Joe:* What's the matter with the roof?
*Harry:* It fell on the dog.
*Joe:* It *fell on the dog*?
*Harry:* After the hurricane.
*Joe:* What hurricane?
*Harry:* I can't help it if you don't tune in the Weather Watch.

Now this made-up dialogue is mildly amusing, but it can be tightened considerably, as follows:

> *Harry:*   Hi Joe.
>
> *Joe:*   Hi, Harry. Nice morning.
>
> *Harry:*   If you say so.
>
> *Joe:*   Well, it *is* a nice morning, isn't it? How are you?
>
> *Harry:*   I'm OK, except for the roof.
>
> *Joe:*   What's the matter with the roof?
>
> *Harry:*   It fell on the dog in the hurricane.
>
> *Joe:*   It *fell on the dog in the hurricane?* What hurricane?
>
> *Harry:*   The one that leveled your house. I can't help it if you don't tune in the Weather Watch.

As you'll notice, while I was tightening our *working example*, something new developed that gave it a dramatic point. In the course of cutting out some of what these two said on their way to saying something important, I discovered what that something important was.

I can't say it often enough: *Revising the way we say things, we find out what we have to say.*

## Rule Three: Dialogue Should Be Dramatic, Not Expository

The best way to demonstrate this is to go back to Joe and Harry and show you what dialogue should *not* do. Let's say that Joe and Harry are back at that first exchange in which Joe says, "Hi, nice morning." Let's say I want my reader to know a number of things I haven't managed to get in until now and I think I can do it by shoveling everything into my dialogue. The scene begins:

> *Harry:*   Hi Joe. Even though we have been working side by side in this office for the last twenty years and you are the success and I am the failure and I'm worried about you getting the Finkle account and causing me to lose my job, I still have to say hello to you.
>
> *Joe:*   Hello, Harry. Even though I spent last night running specs on the Finkle job which I think

> I'm going to lose, I manage to stay cheerful so
> I'm going to say, Nice morning.

Although that particular rendition has a kind of antic charm, it's off the point of the scene. If we need to know these things about these characters, and although I just made them up it's clear we probably do, there are better ways to render them.

> When Harry came into the office, Joe was already at his desk, looking as if he'd been there all night, probably nailing the Finkle account. He had never liked Joe, in spite of which he had to say, "Hi Joe."
> "Hello, Harry." Although he was the office star, Joe envied Harry his good looks, which meant he had to smile particularly brightly, saying, "Nice morning," although as far as he was concerned, it wasn't.

But you will notice that as I cleaned up the speeches, returning them to their simpler form, I discovered yet another new development. Although Joe is the success, he resents Harry because Harry is good looking and Joe isn't.

## *Rule Four: Attributions — Keep It Simple*

Naturally as your characters play their scenes, you want readers to know who's talking. Some beginning writers do this in spades, tagging every speech with some variation of he-said-she-said. Because they're beginners, they're likely to go overboard in finding original and inventive ways to say this: for instance, he or she expostulated/ averred/ added/ explained/ questioned/ remarked/ added.. .etc., etc. You name it. Too many beginning writers have characters *doing* speeches: "Come in," she beamed, or "That's very nice," he smiled, when in fact *beaming* or *smiling* or *laughing* words is a physical impossibility.

Remember:

1. There is absolutely nothing the matter with saying, *she said*.

2. If only two people are talking, you don't need to make

attributions more than once every five or six lines. We can keep track of at least that much in our heads.

3. You can also make attributions by giving stage directions, supplying hand gestures or expressions. Let's look at our *working example*.

> When Harry came into the office, Joe was already at his desk, looking as if he'd been there all night, probably nailing the Finkle account. He had never liked Joe, in spite of which he had to say, "Hi Joe."
>
> "Hello, Harry." Although he was the office star, Joe envied Harry his good looks, which meant he had to smile particularly brightly, saying, "Nice morning," although as far as he was concerned, it wasn't.
>
> Harry smirked. "If you say so."
>
> "Well, it *is* a nice morning, isn't it?" Because he had never liked Harry and couldn't afford to show it, Joe had to smile through gritted teeth and add, "How are you?"
>
> "I'm OK, except for the roof."
>
> "What's the matter with the roof?"
>
> Harry could not stop smiling. "It fell on the dog in the hurricane."

Notice that you and I are altogether clear about who's talking at all times, and that nowhere in this example did I find it necessary to use any of the usual attributions—not even the simple and honorable "he said."

## Rule Five: If in Doubt, Read It Aloud

Most writers working on dialogue can be caught muttering under their breaths or replaying speeches in their heads. Some will even get up from the desk or shift in the chair as they do all the voices and act out all the parts. This is because these are people they are dealing with, and not chairs or tables or ideas. Perhaps the best way to find out whether your characters are talking like real people is to take a deep breath and read each dialogue scene aloud.

More than one actor or actress has reduced a playwright to

tears by refusing to make a speech that is humanly impossible — because the playwright has written a flowery or complex speech that is quite simply unsayable. Reading aloud demonstrates to you whether the words you have put in the mouths of your characters sound like the things people actually say.

## Rule Six: Characters Should Sound Like Individuals

To be be specific, your characters should sound like themselves and not like each other. Again, reading aloud is going to help you identify this problem.

Once you've identified it, there are a couple of things you need to do.

First get firmly back into character and *listen hard*. Your old lady isn't going to sound like your college student, and your southern farmhand isn't going to sound like a businessman from the North. Listen carefully and you will probably hear them. If you don't, then look at what you have on the page and weigh their word choices carefully. Your old lady is likely to deal in euphemisms and not use contractions very often. She's likely to say she "perspires" instead of sweats; she thinks people are "disagreeable," a dated word that nails her age group on the spot. College vocabularies change from year to year but we all know what the speech rhythms are and some things have more or less passed into the language. The southern farmhand is going to say, "Hey," instead of "Hi," will probably use ain't, and the northern businessman? If you don't know any, you'll probably find the diction of any newscaster is going to be close to the mark.

Now, test your characters' speech patterns against the rhythms and word choices of people you know. If your characters sound like people you know, you can't go far wrong.

## Rule Seven: Good Dialogue Is Transactional

The transaction completed can be as simple as Joe and Harry recognizing and re-affirming the fact that they really don't like each other or as complicated as a pair of lovers deciding to break up. Essentially this rule sums up what good dialogue is: it is *action*, dramatic and not expository. Yes, a straight line exists. You can trace it and pull it tight, as characters move from point A to point B.

Think of a dialogue exchange as one in which *something happens*. It takes two people to make a dialogue, and the interplay between characters gives it direction and shape—it is a *transaction*. You are marking the path of the transaction—with each party stating terms.

In some cases, the transaction is completed. Whether or not the transaction is completed is very much up to you as author and your individual characters *as long as the possibility for the transaction exists*.

You have set up the possibility, and part of the tension in any scene is going to be discovering whether things work out the way your characters hope they will. It helps to know that most characters want different things, which means that even in our *working example* between the mythical Harry and Joe you have the added drama of people at cross purposes. If the emotional deal doesn't come off, you have frustration, which has a dramatic power of its own.

Enough. With these simple rules, it's possible for you to go back to a piece of fiction you've written or are writing and apply the following checklist.

## CHECKLIST IV. QUESTIONS ABOUT DIALOGUE

1.  Is something happening in this scene?
2.  Will what's happening be clear to readers through what my characters say?
3.  Can I draw a dramatic line through a scene, demonstrating that they've moved emotionally from point A to point B?
4.  Is this dialogue going to benefit from judicious cutting?
5.  Do these speeches make it clear what's going on in the scene or do I need to clarify or further develop by adding

a few lines?

6. Have I overloaded my speeches by trying to sneak in expository details?
7. Is it clear who's speaking in each case?
8. Are my attributions klunky and unnatural or are they unobtrusive?
9. Can I better use my external attributions to advance the action or demonstrate my speakers' states of mind?
10. When I read aloud, do these people sound like real people?
11. Do they sound like each other or do they sound like individuals?
12. Can I intensify or sharpen what they're saying to each other by making a stronger or more individual choice of words?
13. Have I set down the terms of a transaction in this scene:
    a. By letting my characters set down their own terms?
    b. By showing where they diverge?

If you've gotten into your characters' heads and listened to the way they talk, chances are your dialogue will stand up well to this kind of close scrutiny even in a first draft. The wonderful thing about dialogue is that writing it does come more or less naturally to most writers. It's—yes, as natural as speech—which means that any refining or improving done in the course of revision is fine-tuning of the kind that sharpens scenes and makes them exciting, effective and true.

If your characters are in trouble, then it's time to stop and revise.

## HOW TO PROCEED

First you're going to see whether your dramatic line is clear: what you need to put in or take out to define the movement between point A and point B. If it's not, there are steps you can take.

1. *Tighten.* You'll begin by cutting, going through and get-

ting rid of excess—places where speakers repeat themselves, or where two lines will do the work of four. Learn to take shortcuts between strong, functioning lines, like A: I love you. B: Get out. If the characters have said too much between speech A and speech B, cut or compress.

Cutting is simple. Compression means making one speech do the work of two. For instance, if one character says, "I love you," the second says, "Really?" and the first says, "Really. Ever since the first day I saw you," it's easy to shorten the sequence by having the first speaker say: "I've loved you since the first day I saw you." You've made one line out of three.

Get rid of any extra phrases or word choices that ruin the rhythm or get between your character and the point. Get rid of any unnecessary attributions. If we already know who's talking, we don't need to be told again and again.

2. *Sharpen.* Then you'll go back, line by line, to be certain your characters are saying exactly what you want them to say. They may not be saying what they *mean*, but the intentions behind each speech should be clear to you.

3. *Intensify.* Fill in the gaps. If you've cut away everything that does not apply, you're going to have extra space to move around in. Be certain that your characters are saying *enough* to each other. This doesn't mean spelling things out. It means giving the reader enough information to carry the dramatic business of the scene.

4. *Fine tune.* This means more reading aloud, or replaying the speeches in your head to make certain the word choices and rhythms are exactly as you want them.

As you test and revise your dialogue passages, *making each scene as good as you can make it,* you'll find that major story decisions have taken care of themselves.

*CHAPTER 9*

---

# FOCUS AND BALANCE: POINT OF VIEW, SHOWING VS. TELLING

AS YOU GET MORE AND MORE COMFORTABLE with the elements of fiction — the tools you use to build a story — you'll discover you're ready to move on to more complex considerations.

The first is *focus*. Do all the signposts in your story point in the right direction? That is, does the *way* in which you've written your story tell the reader:

1. What the story is about?
2. Which is the big moment?
3. How to feel about it?

The second is *balance*. Have you *gotten rid of everything that does not function in your story* in order to highlight what's important?

Your selection of point of view and decisions about where to use description and where to demonstrate in scenes both sharpen focus and create a good balance.

## POINT OF VIEW

As you sit down to write, and as you sit down to revise, you need to ask yourself: Do I as writer of this story or novel know where to stand? This means establishing a consistent point of view. To

96

maintain focus and narrative control, you as author need to write from one particular vantage point.

Unless you're an omniscient narrator, detailing everything each of your characters thinks and feels and, perhaps, pulling the whole thing together with authorial commentary, you're going to need to ask yourself some hard questions about point of view.

If you're writing a first-person narration, this is relatively simple. Your character says, I did this/did that/am doing this/will do that. Because you're speaking in your character's voice, you know what that person sees and hears and you tell it *as that person would tell it*. All you need to do is keep it consistent.

The third person offers a number of options:

1. You can use your viewpoint character like a camera, observing only what that character can see and hear or think or remember.

2. You can be a fly on the wall, observing everything everybody does and says but, like that fly, you're going to know what these people *think* only through their actions and what they have to say to each other.

3. You can be omniscient, knowing all and telling all, but remember, the risks are enormous:
    a. Loss of control. Trying to tell *all*, you may lose track of your central story.
    b. Loss of focus. It's a little like trying to keep the audience's eye on one particular performer in a three-ring circus.

4. You can employ multiple viewpoints. Some very good stories intercut first- and third-person narration, giving an overview in third person and then bringing various characters front and center for monologues. Again, the potential for loss of control and focus grows as your story spreads.

Although many novels and some successful stories employ multiple points of view, it's wise for beginning writers to keep it simple. You need to know whether you can control a simple story before you try juggling several points of view in a more ambitious one.

If you're just beginning to write fiction, it's a good idea to choose one method—first- or third-person narration, and if you're writing third-person narration, choose one character as your point-of-view character or "camera."

Picking up one of those collections of "Best" short stories, analyze several for point of view. Reading, ask yourself:

1. What is the point of view here? Is it written in the:
   a. First person.
   b. Second person ("you" do this and that in a story—a risky mode that's becoming more common).
   c. Third person with point-of-view or "camera" character.
   d. Third person "fly-on-the-wall."
   e. Third person omniscient.
   f. Or does it contain multiple points of view? If so, see who the viewpoint characters are, and how many. Try to figure out how the author made the decision. Notice how the author makes the shifts from one viewpoint to another. Does multiple viewpoint enhance or damage the story?
2. Does the point of view pull me, as reader, into the story?
3. If I were retelling this story, what viewpoint would I choose?
4. Which of these viewpoints am I most comfortable with?

Having studied established writers' use of point of view, you're ready to examine your own stories. Reading for revision, ask:

1. Is my narrative told from a definite point of view? As author, where do I stand? Am I omniscient, or have I taken the point of view of a first-person narrator? A third-person character who becomes the point-of-view character?

2. Am I consistent? Do I stay with my point-of-view character or have I jumped into some other character's head? If so, how can I give the reader the same information about that second character without leaving the head of my viewpoint character?

3. Am I playing according to the rules? If you're telling your story in first person, or with a third-person point-of-view character, you're entitled to know *only as much as that character*

*knows*. Any excursions into the heads of secondary characters disrupt the narrative and diffuse focus.

4. If I am telling this story in alternating first- and third-person prose, or using several first-person narrators, is this piece of fiction *long* enough to support more than one narrative point of view? Some writers like to tell stories through more than one narrator, or to intercut first-person narration with third-person accounts. Everything is technically possible, but you as writer need to think carefully about what you have on the page and to be willing to change tactics if multiple viewpoints are going to distract your reader or pull your story apart.

Multiple viewpoints are difficult to bring off in any case, but it's particularly hard to use multiple viewpoints and still maintain focus in a short piece. If your multiple-viewpoint story seems to fly apart under close scrutiny, it's probably a good idea to try to retell it through one of the characters — or to pull back and become the omniscient narrator, taking the reader by the hand through the thicket of your story.

5. Is this piece of fiction *strong* enough to support more than one narrative point of view? This is a question you may have to put to your first reader. If the story carries in spite of the diffuse narrative method, i.e., if it's strong and clear in spite of shifting points of view, then your first reader is going to "get it" and tell you so. If not, it's time to pull back and think about another narrative strategy.

6. If I do decide to alternate viewpoints — first- and third-person narration, for instance, or cuts between two or more first-person narrators — *am I signaling the reader where the narrative is located after each shift?*

There are several ways to do this: through space breaks or sections named for characters, places or times, or through something in the text that makes it clear who's talking, some internal reference that identifies the new viewpoint character in each section — as that character takes over the narrative.

## SHOWING VS. TELLING

Having sharpened focus by establishing a consistent point of view, you can make your story even more effective by considering the relationship in the story between showing and telling.

Most fiction is made up of scenes and description. Authors *describe* or *tell*:

1. What people or places look and sound and feel like.
2. What's going on inside characters' heads.
3. What's happening along the way from the last scene to the next scene.

Through the use of scenes—units in which characters say or do something, acting and interacting, authors *demonstrate* or *show*.

The temptation, particularly for beginning writers, is to tell too much. Because dramatic scenes are often emotionally complicated and tricky to write, they're inclined to chicken out on the big moments, giving the reader "Harry and Martha had a fight," instead of showing the two characters in violent confrontation.

*Showing too much* can be just as bad for your story. If the characters bound and rebound from one fight to another to a third, every fight begins to sound like every other fight and the drama is diffused before the reader ever gets to the big one.

Good writers use both showing and telling, and work hard to strike a balance. A safe rule of thumb for beginners is to cut back on telling and *show* more than you *tell*, but eventually, you're going to want to use both.

*Showing*—demonstrating through action and dialogue passages, you keep the thread of the story tight.

Effective *telling* can enhance drama and prepare the reader for the story's big moments. Although the effectiveness of telling depends in part on how good a writer you are, too much telling can distract your reader, who may lose track out of confusion or, worse, boredom and indifference.

As you revise, ask yourself:

1. Am I describing too much of the action instead of letting it happen in fully rendered scenes?

2. If I'm telling too much, can I let some of it emerge in dialogue exchanges between characters, or by putting my characters in action in some other way?

3. If I'm telling more than is necessary, do I need to cut back? The answer is built into the question. You do.

Be prepared to get rid of passages that come *between* scenes—the kind of detail in which your character gets up and dresses and drives to the office, where the scene you're heading toward is actually going to take place.

Take a clue from the movies. You don't have to show us a character arriving, or tell us what that character does in his spare time between the last major scene and the next. Just cut from one day to the next.

Never tell when you can show. If you have a lethargic character, instead of describing this person at length, give us this character rolling out of the rumpled bed and tripping over the half-empty candy box, demonstrating the effort it takes for this person to move through stages of sleep back to life—or work. If two characters hate each other, don't tell us; let us see them fight.

When in doubt, cut. Even if you as writer are heavily committed to a long descriptive passage that doesn't advance your story, let it go. Chances are your readers won't miss it.

Looking at your story one more time, ask yourself these questions about focus:

1. Is the viewpoint consistent?
2. Am I telling too much?
3. If so, do I need to demonstrate with fresh scenes, cut description, or both?

Once you've been writing for a while, you'll be thinking about all these elements—and all the other elements, which are essentially inseparable, and all part of the same process—more or less at the same time, *from the moment you sit down to write.*

Even when you've gained control of your work, however, you're going to find there's still work to do. This will be true for you this year and every year for as long as you keep on writing; it will be true whether you're a draft writer who's taken a story through several drafts or a sentence-by-sentence writer who's taken weeks or months or even years to arrive at what looks like a final version.

It's the moment at which writer as insider has to move outside the work for one more sharply critical examination.

The time has come to read one more time, making one more revision to judge the success of your work in terms of story and structure.

## CHAPTER 10

# READING FOR STORY AND STRUCTURE

No matter how you work, you won't know for sure whether your work of fiction is doing what you want it to until you think it's finished. You have to believe it's finished before you can really step outside and try to see it the way others do.

Now that you think it's finished, it's time for another look. You need to reread and if necessary revise to make certain the story you carried in your head for so long has made it to the page all in one piece. You want to make it as strong as you can make it before you send it out.

You're ready to move on to the third major kind of revision, which I described in Chapter Three—revising to strengthen story and perfect structure. I've saved details for now because this crucial kind of revision has to wait for until you have the entire story or novel essentially complete.

Now that you have the whole thing, you're ready to consider it as a whole. This makes it possible for you to see more clearly whether you are indeed telling a story and whether or not the story comes off. Is there something at stake here? Does the tension build and is it satisfactorily resolved? Does it hit the mark or fall short? Why? *Have I done it right?*

These are questions you should be asking as you write. You may even be the kind of writer who proceeds best from a detailed outline of events, working with a roadmap designed to take you from point A to point B. If you're a draft writer you'll be able to ask yourself questions about story and structure after each draft, but you'll still have to ask them *one more time*.

By this time you've worked your way through all the other checklists and, armed with a sense of what's right developed through reading and revision, you're ready for the hardest question of all.

*Is it all there?*

There are many things to consider. Story and structural concerns are so tightly interwoven that I'm going to present them within a single extensive checklist with several sections.

# CHECKLIST V: QUESTIONS ABOUT STORY AND STRUCTURE

## Part 1: Action

1. *Is this a story?* By now you've read enough stories to know whether or not you're telling a real story. If you're rereading a novel, the questions become more complex. You may need to read chapter for chapter to see whether individual chapters have *dramatic unity*, that is, to find out whether *something is happening* in each chapter. Then you're going to have to reread the whole and ask yourself whether there is a central story question pulling your reader through the novel as a whole. You're reading for *narrative tug* — the kind of suspense that gives the reader some stake in the outcome. Remember, you're trying to hold reader attention for what may turn out to be hundreds of pages.

If you can't answer this tough question with an immediate *yes*, then ask yourself:

a. Is there something going on here, or is this simply a static description of a situation? Novelists in particular may lose track of this. You may be satisfied with the dramatic shape of individual chapters. Now it's time to read again to be certain there is a unifying concern that makes this a novel and not a series of short stories or, worse, stories and sketches trying to pass themselves off as a novel.

b. If there's supposed to be something going on, have I dramatized this for the reader in scenes or have I only summarized?

c. Is it clear what's at stake here? There should be suspense created, some question raised and answered. Novelist Jessamyn West called this "will-he-won't-he."

d. Have I made clear what my characters care about—what each of them *wants* and how far they're willing to go to get it? Everybody wants something. It's up to you to find out what your characters want and make your readers want it for them.

e. Does my reader have a stake in the outcome? Remember as writer that you can't expect your readers to care about something you don't care about yourself.

2. *Does my setup lead to a payoff?* Some people write beautiful setups—openings lush with description, living, breathing characters—only to shortcut by sketching the end in a few lines, or skipping it altogether, leaving the outcome to the reader's imagination. This may seem subtle, but it's not. Instead it's a symptom of authorial laziness. Be certain to deliver the payoff. This means letting the reader know what you have in mind—completing your own story with the collision of wills or the realization or reconciliation that you had in mind all the time. You may want to end with a BIG MOMENT. If so, be sure it's completely developed so your readers recognize it. *Remember, readers know only what you tell them.*

3. *Have I given enough information so my reader can see what I see?* You don't need to be obvious, but you do need to complete your thinking. You need to supply enough detail to let the attentive reader know what you're getting at, providing insight into characters' motives and background for their dreams. You knew what effect you were trying to create—what you thought you were doing when you wrote this story. Now you're trying to decide whether you've brought it off. This means asking yourself whether the reader is going to be able to make out your intentions. Ask:

a. Is my reader, who is essentially a stranger to this story, going to be able to tell what's going on between these characters I know so well?

b. Have I introduced story strands that I haven't tied up? If so, you may need to rework the section in question or the whole story, making sure that the shotgun you brought onstage in the first scene is fired in the last, and if it isn't, that there's a foolproof explanation of the reasons why.

c. Have I drawn and dramatized all the major events or do some of my biggest moments happen offstage? If so, can I develop further to make my work stronger?

## Part 2: Consistency

Making certain this story or novel you've written is all of a piece, that it does what it sets out to do, you're going to need to ask yourself certain technical questions.

1. Have I been faithful to point of view?
2. What about the time scheme?
    a. Does my story begin at the beginning? As I've suggested in the chapter on dialogue, sometimes we write a lot on the way to finding out what we have to write. Now is the time to take out the excess. If your first scene begins with a lengthy description of setting *that does nothing to advance the story*, chances are it needs to be cut or tightened. Ask: Does my story really begin here? If you can free yourself of commitment to what you've already written, you may be able to *cut to the chase*. If starting here necessitates a lot of explanation or klunky flashbacks, keep asking: Does my story begin here or earlier or later? Where?
    b. Does a complex time scheme help or hurt here? If you're using flashbacks to avoid the had-hads, judge yourself harshly. Ask yourself: how much of this information is important to the story? How much can I suggest or imply in other ways, and how much can I do without?
    c. Can I cut down on the number of shifts? Sometimes telescoping flashbacks—joining two segments of time past to cut down on trips back and forth to the present—can strengthen the time present story line and make it more effective.
    d. Am I shifting in time at the right point? If you're alternating between past and present, is there a logic to the shifts—when you go from present into the past, and when you shift back?
    Is the past line chronological, and if not, why not? Can you justify the chronology? Is there a valid reason for

the story to shuttle back and forth between points in
the past?

e.  Am I making it clear on the page when time shifts
occur? There are many ways of signaling this, from
the use of space breaks and section labels to tag lines
that pull the reader into a section. As you're asking
for close attention, you'd better be sure you've given
adequate direction markers.

f.  Is the chronology clear? Even patient readers need
something to go on — the sense that if they follow you
faithfully, they're going to find out not only where
they are, but *when* they are.

3.  What about the tone? It's possible to intercut comic and
tragic sections in a novel and have the thing work as a
whole, but it's harder to do in a short story. No matter
how complex the time scheme or use of tense or point
of view, you want your story or novel to look as if it is all
written by the same person.

## Part 3: Completeness

This is hard for most of us to see without outside help, because
the work we've just finished is always the one closest to our
hearts. We know it so well that we can't see why everybody else
won't too. We've lived with our characters so long that we assume our readers have too.

Now it's time to try to see them through the eyes of a reader
who's never met them. We have to be alert to gaps so we can
supply what's missing — what we see that the reader can't. An
outside reader unfamiliar with the piece can be particularly
helpful here.

1.  Is my story all there? I know what I'm trying to do, but
is everybody else going to?

2.  Have I skimped on exposition, assuming my reader's
going to know what I know?

3.  Have I left too much to my reader's imagination? Even
the best readers need a few signposts — descriptive details to set
the scene, indications through dialogue, characters' aspect (that

is, carriage or expression) or action to let them know what characters have on their minds.

4. Have I skipped key scenes? Some writers lose their big moments by lapsing into summary—others just leave them out. "You mean you didn't *know* he was in love with his sister?" Instead of berating the reader who doesn't "get it," reread to see what you've left out.

## Part 4: Pacing

This is a big consideration, and your answers are going to be determined in large part by how attentive you've been to all the matters of action, consistency and completeness. Whether you've just finished a short story or a novel, you're going to need to ask yourself some of the same questions.

- Does my story take too long to get started?
- Are the individual scenes dramatic?
- Is the whole dramatic?
- Is there a big enough payoff at the ending to justify what precedes it?
- What about the balance between showing and telling? Have I demonstrated all my big moments with scenes or have I only summarized?
- Do I need to cut description or summary to heighten the effect of my scenes?
- Is my reader going to be satisfied that *something important has happened here*?
- Does it end in the right place or did I keep on writing after I should have written "the end?"

Because a novel is a long and complicated work, you'll want to go through, chapter for chapter, asking yourself these questions about each unit. Then you're going to have to try and stand back from the work as a whole so you can see whether the entire piece is in balance—whether your long narrative, made up of individual dramatic units, starts in the right place, moves fast and pulls the reader along to the ultimate big moment.

As you begin a novel, all through the long job and now at this last reading, try to keep in mind what's at stake in the novel as a whole. You can't tell readers everything right away but you do want them to stay with you through however many individual episodes there are, for however many pages it takes you to let them know the outcome. Two things are particularly useful here:

1. *The chapter hook*: the immediate question raised to draw the reader from one chapter to the next. What's going to happen next?
2. *The larger narrative question*: What's going to happen at the end of this whole book?

You want your readers to wonder — and care.

## Part 5: Length

It's important to tighten so your readers can keep track of the questions you've raised. You may already have that uncomfortable suspicion that your work is too long, and you may know which section needs cutting or compressing, in which case it's time to sit down with the pencil or marker and get to work.

If you're still not sure, ask yourself: is my story too long for what it does?

Your sense of this is going to depend largely on your ability to step back from what you've done and judge it according to the same high standards you apply to fiction you've read. Try to be objective when you answer the next questions.

1. Is it boring? I know this is a hard question, and if you try and try and still can't answer it honestly for yourself, ask a reader you trust.

2. Does too much detail in one section ruin the proportion? An example: You've spent the first three pages of a ten-page story describing the farmhouse where the action takes place. Chances are, your story is out of proportion and you need to cut.

3. Does this section function in the story? To know this, you'll need to be able to see what you've written as a whole, and you're also going to have to be objective and cold-blooded about it. If you're in doubt, remove the pages in question, set them

aside and try reading the piece without them. Then give it to someone else to read. It's going to be clear whether you need the section in question or not.

## Part 6: Organization

Intelligent cutting enhances organization. It's like pruning a tree to make it take its proper shape. Unlike trees, fiction can also be rearranged.

You're showing readers what you think is most important by deciding what to put first.

The longer the work, the more complicated questions of organization are going to be, quite simply because it's harder to stand off from it and get a good look. A short story can go as badly wrong as a novel, but because it's short, its problems are easier to identify and correct.

Even though novels are more complex, you'll discover that in most cases organizational revision does not involve an enormous amount of new writing, or rewriting. Instead it is a matter of being able to divide the work into units and step back and try to see whether in this draft, the units fall in the right place.

You can judge your narrative for organization:

1. According to standards you've developed through reading.
2. With the help of a reader.
3. By applying a simple test.

The technique I suggest applies to both short and long fiction. This simple method can help you locate and identify problems of organization. It offers a low-fault method of trying out different solutions.

This technique can also be applied on the job, as you approach the end of a piece the first time through. Student writers I know have used it successfully to find out how to finish long pieces, making tactical decisions about the end of a story or a novel on a trial-and-error basis *by moving items on a list*. It will not tell you what kinds of things to put in or leave out but it will help you develop a surer sense of where they belong. This is how it works.

1. Break down your piece by making a list. List the major events or units—not in detail, but in two or three words. I'm not talking here about naming chapters, but rather, events, or sequences.

If you'd written *The Great Gatsby*, for instance, the first few items on the list might look like this:

   Nick meets Gatsby
   Nick's feelings for Daisy
   first party

Each item stands for something complicated and each falls into the narrative in a certain order. You should be able to find appropriate labels for major events in anything you've written, no matter how ambitious.

2. Now look at the order.

3. Rearrange the items on your list. Remember, this is a very small investment of time compared to what you've already spent. It's also a low-risk way of trying out alternative solutions. Remember, this is only a list. So far, your story or novel is intact; you haven't changed a word.

4. Keep rearranging items until you're satisfied that the order is right. If it's what you started out with, this is nature's way of telling you that structurally, your piece is as well put-together as you can make it.

5. If you find the list of elements has settled in a different order from the one you started out with, go back to your story or novel and reorganize and revise accordingly.

6. If you do your job carefully and are willing to be flexible about approaching reorganization; if you're willing to spend some time considering and weighing each piece *and* its place, the natural order should assert itself.

7. If you put everything in its right place and find you have some units or items left over because they don't belong in the

new order, take a deep breath and put them aside.

8. Now it's time to go back and read for consistency, especially if your revision has altered the time scheme. If this means making phrase changes or writing connective paragraphs, be prepared to do them.

Once you've responded to all the questions on this last, major checklist for yourself, you've done the hardest part—reading to find out where and how your story and structure need revision.

## SUMMARY CHECKLIST

1. Is it a story?
2. Have I made it accessible to my reader?
3. Am I consistent in my use of point of view, time scheme and tone?
4. Is my story complete or do I need to develop it further?
5. What about the pace? Does it move swiftly or have I slowed it down by too much telling and not enough showing?
6. Does it need cutting?
7. What about the organization? Is it unfolding in the right order?

Making decisions about what's working and what's not working and what to do about it is the hard part.

The easy part is carrying them out.

We'll talk about nuts and bolts—the physical ways to deal with and complete revision—in the next chapter.

## CHAPTER 11

# HOW TO PROCEED

BY THIS TIME YOU PROBABLY have plenty of ideas about what you intend to do to a story or novel that needs revision.

There is one last item we need to talk about before we move on into ways to make words and phrases and entire scenes end up where you want them to. This consideration demonstrates as well as any the link between thought and the physical business of carrying out revision. It is cutting.

## CUTTING VS. COMPRESSION

We all develop a sense of which passages in our stories or novels are too long for what they do. If we don't know this instinctively, there's usually a reader or an editor who will point it out to us.

In some cases, it's simply a matter of removing a scene or a paragraph of description or an entire section that doesn't work and isn't necessary. In other cases, what we're doing is OK, it's simply too long for what it does. We are going to have to make it shorter.

There are two ways to approach this:

1. *Cutting.* We either draw a line through or erase parts of the passage, eliminating words to make it shorter.

2. *Compression.* We rewrite or retype the passage to make it shorter. We're not so much cutting as changing the prose in the passage to boil it down—we're trying to say exactly the same

things in the same way, but in a way that makes the passage shorter and tighter.

I'll invent a verbose passage and then show you two ways of making it shorter.

> In the autumn of the first year after she was married to Jerome in a summer ceremony with only Jerome's mother and sister in attendance, Marguerite had a very bad time getting along with her husband Jerome's family. It wasn't that she didn't like her husband's mother Mary and his sister Eleanor, who had a wen on her nose and always walked around in work boots and support stockings, it was simply that the two women got on Marguerite's nerves because they wandered around the house—Marguerite's house!—in their country clothes with their faces fixed in faintly negative expressions that to Marguerite, at least, suggested they were feeling disapproval.

First let me edit with a pencil, showing you how this would look if I simply cut out some words and phrases to make it shorter.

> In the autumn of the ~~first~~ year after she ~~was~~ married ~~to~~ Jerome, ~~in a summer ceremony with only Jerome's mother and sister in attendance,~~ Marguerite had a ~~very~~ bad time getting along with *his* ~~her husband Jerome's~~ family. It wasn't that she didn't like ~~her husband's~~ *his* mother Mary and his sister Eleanor, who had a wen on her nose and ~~always~~ walked around in work boots and support stockings, ~~it was simply that~~ The two women got on Marguerite's nerves because they wandered around *her* ~~the~~ house—~~Marguerite's house!~~—in their country clothes with their faces fixed in ~~faintly negative~~ expressions that ~~to Marguerite, at least,~~ suggested ~~they were feeling~~ disapproval.

It's clear that I can get rid of a lot of verbiage that way, but as a writer more accustomed to compression, I seem to need to *re-write*, not so much cutting as compressing.

> In the autumn after she married Jerome with only his

mother and sister present, Marguerite had trouble getting along with them. It wasn't that she disliked Mother Mary or Eleanor, who clomped around in work boots and support stockings, it was just that she found them unnerving, wandering around the house—Marguerite's house!—in their country clothes with fixed expressions of faint disapproval.

Remember, this is only an example constructed to demonstrate method. None of these versions is going to win any prizes, but versions two and three are definitely shorter than the first, and I would submit that the third is smoother than the other two.

Cutting your own work, you may settle on a combination of cutting and compression, crossing out words and then rewriting to make a smoother, shorter version.

Now you're ready for the final consideration—which tools and which methods you're going to use to make your revision.

Looking at your work, judging it according to standards you've developed through reading and asking yourself some of the questions on the appropriate checklists, you've made certain decisions about what needs cutting or compressing, what needs changing, what organizational changes need to be made. Once you've made the artistic decisions, only mechanical choices remain.

Now it's time to get down to nuts-and-bolts considerations—how to make the best use of your tools of the trade. By this time you probably know whether you're most at home writing by hand or on a typewriter or a computer, or using some combination of the three. Even with the major decisions already made, you may find the idea of getting all the right words in the right place somewhat daunting.

This is a good time to let method take over. If you know *where* you're going to do a revision and *what* you need to do, it helps to develop a few working habits. Knowing *how* you're going to do something makes it easier to get started. There are no shortcuts, but there are some mechanical techniques that make the physical business of revision easier.

## THE NOTEBOOK

If you compose with pen or pencil, you've already developed a couple of systems—crossing out or replacing words, X-ing out sections and marking sections you want to move from one place to another. You also know that at a certain point you need to copy the whole thing over so you can read what you've written and that either you or a professional typist is going to have to make a typescript.

Once you have a typescript you're likely to want to make more pen changes and have a corrected typescript made. Before you submit your manuscript to an editor, you'll need to have a clean copy of the entire work, typed or printed double-spaced with pages accurately numbered and your name and address on the title page.

There are several tricks you can play on yourself to make composing easier and help yourself get started on revisions.

1. Even when writing by hand, double or triple space. Leave margins where you can. This gives you more room for the notes, expansions, word changes and additions of phrases you're going to make as your story develops.

2. A loose-leaf notebook will make organization easier. You can move entire sections and add, expand or remove scenes without having to recopy the entire story or chapter each time you want to change something.

3. Using a loose-leaf notebook, you can add pages of notes or outline pages as you make them, and move them as necessary without disrupting your text.

4. In some cases you may be able to cut and paste, taping four or five replacement lines over the original text, or cutting the page in two so you can insert a new scene. This makes it possible to make changes as you go without having to recopy. If you use both sides of the page, cut up a photocopy.

5. When your text gets too messy to be legible, it's nature's way of telling you it's time to copy the whole thing over. You'll find developmental changes and ideas for expansion occur as you go.

6. There is a point when you need to move into typescript. Before you can consider yourself finished, you're going to have to see what you've written in cold, uncompromising type. Because hand-writing is intensely personal, some writers get so committed to the way the page looks in an abstract way—all those loopy Ls and Ys—that they have a hard time seeing what they've written in a cold light. If you can type, move to the typewriter or the computer. If not, pay to have a draft typed with the idea that you're probably going to need to keep revising.

7. If in doubt, copy it over. If you have the vague sense that a scene or an entire piece isn't working right and you don't know what to do about it, recopying is the best way to solve the problem. You'll discover that faulty sentences straighten themselves out and the logic of what you're doing asserts itself as you reproduce it on a fresh page. Dialogues seem to develop and grow. Often the donkey work of copying frees the mind to solve narrative problems.

8. Copy over yesterday's work if you're having a hard time getting started. This is also an excellent way to avoid the mythical writer's block. If you're copying, at least you're *working*, and at some point you'll gather momentum, writing on to discover what's on the next page.

9. Duplicate your manuscript and put the photocopy in a safe place. Notebook writers are inclined to carry their work with them—on buses, planes, taxis, to the beach. Because they're portable and easily damaged by water, manuscripts in notebooks are particularly accident-prone. You're going to want to take this simple step to insure yourself against loss.

## THE TYPEWRITER

I began my career as a writer on a Royal Standard office model—manual. Naturally I became heavily committed to typing as a way of composing—and as a way of life. Composing on the typewriter seemed easier than writing by hand—or making handwritten changes or corrections—because I could always retype to make the page look the way it ought to. As I typed, I discovered the words kept rearranging themselves until they said the right thing.

Along the way, I developed a few techniques for revision that may be useful to anybody who works on a typewriter.

1. Always double or triple space to leave room for changes, expansion or notes. Wide margins are a help for the same reason. Double space your final draft.

2. When in doubt, retype. You are integrating composition and revision. This simple procedure works on sentence drafts, page drafts, completed first drafts. There is a connection between head and hands that allows the brain to keep working and developing your thoughts even as you type. This is one of the best and most significant things about working on a typewriter.

3. Begin the day by retyping the last two or three pages you finished the day before. This gives you continuity. The pages you retype will get better in the process and you'll have a running head start on the new day's work.

4. At the end of each day, sit down with a pen or pencil and look over what you've done. You'll catch typographical errors immediately but, more important, you'll begin to see how your work may change and grow when you get back to it the next morning.

5. If you need to make word changes on what is essentially a finished typescript, you can do it easily, either by retyping (see above) or with the help of White-Out or correction tape.

6. If you need to reorganize:
a. Number the sections that need moving. Put corresponding numbers in the text in the pages where you're going to insert these sections.
b. Cut apart the page in the place where you're going to make the insertions.
c. Use glue or tape to make the reorganization.
d. Retype the affected pages. If you're making large changes in a short story, it makes sense to spend the extra time and retype it from the beginning. You'll need to make your own decisions about longer pieces of fiction. Suffice it

to say that almost every work of fiction benefits from being typed over by the author, from the top, and that potential publishers may be unnecessarily prejudiced by numbering changes on a manuscript that looks as if it's been taken apart and put together again.

7. If you need to cut:

a. Cross out the sections you're doing away with or earmark them for compression.

b. Cut the page to remove the section in question.

c. If you're compressing, you can either retype the page including the compressed paragraph, or cut and paste or tape in the new section to see what it looks like before you retype the page.

8. If you need to make insertions, you can follow the steps listed above. If you're inserting several pages but not retyping the entire manuscript, be sure to renumber all the pages or add A, B, C, etc. to the new pages, as: 28A, 28B, 28C, etc.

9. Most editors don't like corrasable bond because it smudges, but it's the easiest way to make corrections and last-minute word changes and still have a presentable typescript for submission. Corrasable will give you the flexibility to make changes at the last minute. A good, clear photocopy will bypass the editor's prejudice. Most editors will accept *a clear photocopy* so long as you let them know this is not a multiple submission. If this is a big project and you're in any doubt, inquire before you submit.

10. Every time you accumulate a significant number of pages—pages you don't want to have to try to reproduce from memory—have them duplicated. You're not as likely to lose a manuscript as a writer who carries handwritten work around from place to place, but these things do happen. A photocopy also gives you a record of what you had on the page before you began revising. Naturally you'll keep a copy of every finished manuscript you send out for possible publication.

## THE COMPUTER

Notice that I call the instrument in question a computer, not a word processor. Machines don't process words. They don't even work with them. People do. The computer with the so-called word processing program makes the physical process — all those deletions, all that reorganization, all that cutting and pasting — considerably easier. Remember, I say it makes the *physical process* easier. Decisions are just as hard, as is the demanding business of thinking through what you're doing.

Critics like to say that computers lend themselves to automatic writing: all those words, and on a screen, too, and so fast! It's not writing, they say, it's more like TV! Only amateurs think so. Although there's a certain glamour to technology, it's only technology. Think of the computer as a super typewriter, with built-in functions that make it possible for the demanding writer to go back to the text again and again in the attempt to make it *right* — functions that encourage the writer who'd like to think of the work as finished to push each revision even farther.

Everybody knows computers make typing (notice I say typing, and not *writing*) quicker and easier. In spite of the speed of the machine, *it takes me exactly as long to compose on the computer as it did on the typewriter.*

If it takes me just as long to write a story or finish a novel as it ever did, where does the time go? I'd like to think that it goes into development through revision. Instead of typing and re-typing up to seventeen versions of a first sentence to arrive at something that satisfies me, I have the liberty to push to twenty, twenty-five, twenty-eight. Instead of having to spend quite so much time on donkey work, typing and retyping, I have more freedom to think about what I'm doing.

I will never know whether I was at some level calling my typescripts finished before they were really finished because I was physically exhausted from all that retyping, but I do know that it's easier for me to keep grappling with something when the medium is as flexible as the computer. For me, it seems as swift and mobile as thought. I'm thinking and rethinking, organizing and reorganizing on the screen.

Demonstrating my new toy to the poet Richard Wilbur, I showed him how quickly, almost magically I could consider some eight options in the choice of a particular verb. We both agreed this was no way to write poetry, but the mobility — the potential for thinking through, unencumbered by ink and paper — amazed him.

The computer makes me reread everything I do from the top every morning. As an inveterate typist, I used to retype instead of reread. Because typing is long and life is short, I'd redo only the last scene I'd done the day before. Now I begin at the top of the file and page through the story or chapter from the beginning, screen by screen, correcting typos and making small changes and large ones, before I pick up where I left off the day before.

I am fairly certain that the computer has made me more open to possibilities for revision. I can look at a novel I think is finished and see it in terms of what needs to be done without facing the grisly prospect of retyping some 300-plus pages in order to make a presentable-looking manuscript.

In the course of working with beginning student writers, I've made an interesting discovery that suggests that in spite of the fears of its critics, the computer can make us better writers.

The student faced with the prospect of revising a typescript will go to any lengths to defend those perfectly typed pages — *anything to keep from having to retype*.

The student who works on the computer listens carefully to group discussion of a faulty story, says, "Oh, OK," and goes away to see how the story in question ought to be reworked.

I can report firsthand that the computer makes it easier to get started. When I moved from the Royal Standard office model manual, I threw out my scissors and glue and my corrasible and my White-Out. I still go through all the same processes. I work just as hard. Freed from the messy, mechanical business of incorporating changes, I may work even harder.

If you're already composing on a computer, I don't need to describe the advantages of computer over typewriter or my computer over yours, and there's no point in discussing the relative merits of so-called word processing programs. Most of us are committed to our own hardware and software because it was quite simply a case of love at first sight.

If you don't compose on a computer and have managed to avoid the usual prejudices, I suggest that you beg, borrow or rent a session on one with a helping hand from a friend who can show you just exactly how it works. You'll come to your own conclusions and make your own decisions. If you decide to buy one, you'll get plenty of advice about which is a good computer and what is the best program for the kind of work you do from colleagues with computers.

I might even suggest that even though you think you hate and fear computers, you ought to consider making your final typescript on one, for all the above reasons. Even when you think you're finished you may need to revise one more time at the request of an editor. With your work recorded on a disk, you can still take advantage of some of the following tricks for revision.

## Computer Revision

1. Naturally you will begin by storing what you write frequently, and backing up every file with a copy. You may also want to print at the end of every working day. If you work on floppies, copy onto a backup. If you're working on a hard disk, back up with a floppy. Be certain to store and copy all changes at the end of every working session.

2. When you begin revising, you may want to keep at least one copy on disk of every version you write of a story or novel, in addition to a printout. This gives you a permanent record of your progress through various drafts, and enables you to retrieve things you've cut but may decide later that you want to restore.

3. If you're having trouble with a particular passage, copy it into a separate file so you can go back to it and work on it without distractions. You may want to put it through several versions before you replace your original version.

4. If you've learned how to use your word processing program, you already know how to make word changes and how to reorder sentences within paragraphs. You'll use block marking and moving procedures to reorganize the order of paragraphs.

5. You may want to print out at the end of every day's work and revise on hard copy. Moving away from the screen helps distance you from your text in the same way that revising on a typescript helps somebody who writes by hand. It will help you see your piece as a whole. It makes sense to read every finished story or chapter over in hard copy with an eye toward possible revision.

6. When you go to work, page through yesterday's file from the beginning, reading for typographical errors and making necessary word changes as you go.

7. Before you move on, enter the changes you made on hard copy. Using hard copy as a reference, run your FIND function, using a distinctive word or string to take you to each spot where you're making changes.

9. You can use your FIND and REPLACE function to change character or place names throughout. You can also use it to locate distinctive words and phrases — the kind that are too big or unusual to be used more than once, even in a novel. It will also help you eliminate repetitious phrasing. The computer is going to be quick to let you know whether you've already used a word like "bizarre" or whether a phrase like "as she liked to remember" turns up one time too many. Once you've located repetitions, it's easy to make substitutions. Knowing is half the battle.

10. If you're cutting a section or a scene, move it to a specially named file until you're certain you really want to get rid of it. If you know where it is, you can always get it back in case you decide you want to replace it.

11. If you're reorganizing, sometimes it helps to set up a separate file for the passage in question instead of moving it from one place to another only to have to move it again. Once you have it in a file of its own, it's out of the way but you know where to go if you decide you need it.

12. Reading for story and structure, make your list of elements *on the screen*. This gives you flexibility in ordering and re-ordering until you're certain that your organization is the right one.

13. If you think you need to expand a scene, you may want

to copy it onto a separate file and do your revision there, before reading it back into your story or chapter.

14. You can move entire sections or chapters, trying things out first here and then there in order to find out where they sit comfortably. It's wise to keep an unchanged backup.

15. Unless you're a meticulous speller with an infallible eye for typographical errors, wait until you're truly finished and then run your spelling check before you print.

16. Many editors refuse to read products from dot matrix printers. If you don't have a letter quality printer you may want to find one you can use to make your final copy. If none is available, put your dot matrix printer on double strike and photocopy the product. In many cases, editors won't be able to tell the difference, and if they do, they can't really complain because you've done your best to make it immediately legible.

17. Even though you think you've proofread on the screen, proofread on hard copy. For whatever reasons, typographical errors are more obvious once they're on paper.

## WHAT'S NEXT

Once you've read and reread and rewritten your manuscript, asking most of the questions I've suggested in earlier chapters, and taking some of the steps, you've gone as far as you can go without some concrete news from the outside world.

It's time to start sending out your manuscript. You can do this yourself, trying to target your market by learning as much as possible, as I suggested in Chapter Four, or you can look for an agent to offer your work, using tactics I described in Chapter Four.

You will see to it that your manuscript is cleanly typed, double spaced, with the pages numbered, and that your name and address are on the title page. Mail it flat, not folded, and enclose a self-addressed envelope with return postage. Keep a record of where you're sending it, and when, and as a healthy next step, list one or two other places where you might like to send it if this editor rejects it.

And then?

The best thing to do while you're waiting for a response from the outside world—in short, while you're waiting to find out whether or not this bird is going to fly—is to start something new.

You've already done the best job you could on the manuscript you began with. Now you're going to discover an unexpected payoff. An agent I once had put it this way: "Nothing you write is wasted."

*Every time you revise, you learn something about writing.*

This means that you're likely to find that the work goes better on the new story because you've confronted certain artistic problems and found new ways of solving them. This is true after one year of writing, or ten, or a long lifetime. The better you get at writing, at judging what you've written and rewriting, the surer your touch is going to be.

As a result, you're going to develop a stake in the new piece you're writing—and you're likely to turn to it with increased confidence.

Whatever you do, keep working. It's the best way to keep from dying if the response from the outside world this time turns out to be no.

And if your work comes back, not once but several times? You'll look at it one more time, trying to decide whether you can put it over on the next submission—as soon as you rewrite.

Good luck.

# CHAPTER 12

# KNOWING WHEN TO QUIT

BUT YOU'RE STILL HERE. You think your manuscript is ready to go but you want to pass your hands over it one more time before you send it off.

It's time for a quick once-over.

Before you do anything else, ask yourself: Is this a story? Does something *happen* here? Is there the kind of development that makes it clear this is not a sketch or an essay but a story? If you're finishing a novel, ask yourself: Is my central story thread pulled tight enough to hold my reader's attention throughout?

If you're confident that the answer is YES, it's time to move on to the final checklist.

1. Does this begin at the beginning?

2. Is the beginning effective? Will the reader know and care about what's going on here?

3. Have I used enough detail to set the scene and give the reader a sense of what's going on? Have I used the right details? Can I be more specific?

4. Are my characters believable? Would they behave the way they do in this story?

5. Is the dialogue dramatic? Convincing? Characteristic? Do my people sound like real people? Does the dialogue need cutting? Or do I need to develop scenes further?

6. Am I faithful to the point of view I've chosen? If there are multiple points of view, are the shifts clear to the reader?

7. Does the story unfold logically? Is the chronology clear? If there is a complicated time scheme is it justified, and have I made the time shifts clear to the reader?

8. What about focus? Are all the signs pointing in the right direction? Do all the scenes and descriptive passages lead up to and away from the key scene, or big moment?

9. What about organization? Is everything in the right place?

10. Is my story too long for what it does in any section? Do I need to make cuts, or to keep the passages in question but compress for dramatic effect?

11. What about the balance between showing and telling? Am I giving my readers enough scenes or am I describing too much?

12. Am I taking too much for granted? Is the reader going to get the point or do I need to expand?

13. What about narrative tone? Whether it's comic, tragic, a mystery or historical, *does it sound like what it's supposed to be?*

14. Have I proofread?

If you've answered all these questions to your satisfaction, you're ready to mail. Most of you are already reaching for the 8 × 11 envelope.

What about the rest?

At this stage some of you are still holding on to your manuscripts, whether through feelings of anxiety or inferiority or simply because you feel safer fussing endlessly over the same old familiar thing than putting your work out where it will be judged — or starting something new.

For the moment, you may need to cut loose and send out your work before you think you're ready. If you're still doubtful, instead of mailing to an agent or editor, or asking for an outside reading, put it away and *start something new*. Getting into a new piece of work is going to put things into perspective for you. It may even give you the courage to put that much-revised piece before an audience — a key step if you're going to grow as a writer.

Everybody's got to find out the truth sometime. You may be delighted to discover that somebody out there likes your work. What if they don't? There are three things you need to remember:

1. This isn't the only thing you're ever going to write.
2. You won't die if this particular work is a flop.
3. An individual failure is easier to take *if you don't stake everything on one work*. Starting something new is the best insurance I know.

As you write more, you're going to develop the *insider's sense of rightness*. With practice, you're going to be able to keep most of the major artistic questions in your head all at the same time instead of thinking of them as separable elements. The better you get at what you're doing, the more quickly you're going to know whether something's working or not working so you can make sound decisions as you go.

This growing sense of rightness is the ultimate payoff to the time and effort you've spent on writing and revision. It will tell you when to persist and when to quit. It's going to make you feel good about your work.

# *Appendix*

It's clear that one of the best ways to show you how to revise is to let you see how professionals do it. Beginning this book, I asked two writers for manuscript samples of early drafts — and copies of the work as it finally appeared in print.

Lois Gould has published six novels, including *Such Good Friends*, *A Sea-Change* and *La Presidenta*. Manuscript page and page proofs from her newest novel, *Subject to Change*, appear in Chapter Two. Gould has also written nonfiction and originated the *Hers* column for the *New York Times*. Explaining why she composes and revises in longhand, she says, "I always felt punished, chaining myself to a machine with a plug and having it hum reproachfully at me." Her interest in this project prompted The Writers Room exhibit on revision and through her kindness and the cooperation of Renata Rizzo-Harvi, executive director of The Writers Room, we reproduce a portion of it here.

Also reproduced here is the manuscript extract by Thomas M. Disch, discussed in the second chapter. Drama critic for *The Nation*, Disch has published everything from SF and an interactive novel for the computer to poetry. His novels include *Camp Concentration*, the pseudonymous *Clara Reeve* and *The Businessman, a Tale of Terror*.

He is currently working on an adaptation of *Ben Hur* for an off-Broadway company. He says, "I write in longhand in a spiral notebook only when I'm out of the house away from a typewriter."

His extract from a short story titled "Hard Work" is included in the Appendix. It appeared in the British magazine *Interzone*.

The rest of the manuscript samples come from The Writers Room exhibit, which garnered national attention and prompted a series of public readings by the authors included. At Lois Gould's suggestion, the exhibition was organized by executive director Renata Rizzo-Harvi, who has provided the accompanying text.

Although the exhibition included manuscripts by poets and writers of nonfiction as well, the Appendix focuses on manuscript pages of works of fiction and writing for the stage.

Founded in 1978, The Writers Room was designed as an alternative for New York-based writers who had been working in the Frederick Lewis Allen Room at the New York Public Library. The object was to provide office space at low rates on a twenty-four-hour basis.

Any writer with a serious writing project may be considered for admission. Admission is for three months and may be extended. There is a $50 initiation fee due upon acceptance and quarterly fees for writers are $150. The Room, located at 153 Waverly Place in Greenwich Village, welcomes writers from all over the country who are visiting New York and is supported by contributions which are tax deductible.

Here are illustrations of manuscript pages and page proofs indicating first and final drafts by these writers. They are number keyed to details about the authors and discussion of their work habits. The illustrations follow.

Note that no two writers go about revising the same way.

—Kit Reed

Figures 1 and 1a. From *August*, a novel written in The Writers Room by Judith Rossner. Rossner is the author of more than seven novels, including *Attachments*, *Emmeline* and *Looking for Mr. Goodbar*. This is the third draft of the first page of the novel that was to become *August*, part of 100-odd pages that were ultimately "thrown away," the author says, "or at least consigned to a file someplace."

In a departure from her usual method of starting novels on

lined pads, Rossner began her current novel in progress on a computer. After writing 400 pages, however, she discovered that the book's plots were proliferating wildly. "The story was branching out instead of turning into an overwhelming stream," says Rossner. So she closed down her computer and went back to her typewriter to complete the novel. "Using a computer offers you so many possibilities," Rossner says, "and it never forces you to choose between them."

Figures 2 and 2*a*. From a screenplay in progress by James Lapine. Lapine co-authored *Sunday in the Park with George*, and is the writer and director of the Broadway musical *Into the Woods*, for which he recently won a Tony award for Best Book.

Figures 3 and 3*a*. From *Shuffle, Shuffle, Jive, Shuffle*, a play in progress by Ted Bent. Bent has written extensively for magazines, film, television and radio.

Bent generally starts writing on large lined pads, then goes back and forth between longhand and computer. He revises both on the monitor and by printing out copy and making changes in longhand. For a given project, he may write four drafts, with "endless" revisions within each draft. "I find writing on a computer is like writing on water," Bent says. "It's wonderful because it allows endless flexibility in experimenting with changes."

Figures 4 and 4*a*. From a work in progress, *Identity Papers*, by Signe Hammer. Hammer is the author of *Passionate Attachments: Fathers and Daughters in America Today* and *Daughters and Mothers, Mothers and Daughters*.

Hammer begins writing on a computer, and also revises on a computer until she senses that her work is ready to print out. She then makes revisions on hard copy, often seeing things that she didn't catch on the computer screen. These changes are ultimately entered into the computer, and the cycle begins again. "This process can be done several times for one piece of work until I think it's finally finished," Hammer says. "But it never really is."

Figures 5 and 5*a*. From a novel in progress by James Whitfield Ellison. Ellison is the author of seven novels, including *Master Prim*, *Proud Rachel* and *Buddies*.

Ellison begins writing by making longhand notes, which he eventually transfers to a computer. He edits both on the monitor and on hard copy, but feels that final editing is best done on hard copy where he can see the text as it might appear in published form.

Figures 6, 6*a* and 6*b*. From *The Deal*, a play by Matthew Witten, which has been produced in Boston and Philadelphia and which will appear in *Best Plays of 1987-88*. Witten has had eleven plays and musicals produced, and was the First Prize Winner of the 1987 Clauder Competition for Playwrights.

Figures 7 and 7*a*. From "Beholding," a short story by Sheri Stein, who is currently working on a collection of short stories and a novella.

Figures 8 and 8*a*. From *Orchard Song*, a new novel by Lucinda Franks, which is being published by Random House in 1989. Franks, a Pulitzer Prize winner for National Reporting, is the author of *Waiting Out a War*. She is a member of the board of directors of The Writers Room.

Franks wrote *Orchard Song* on a typewriter, making continual revisions on pages. "My revised pages often look like a ten-car pileup with all the carats and cross-outs and inserted words," she says. She is thinking about working on a computer in the future, but has reservations. "I think a lot of novelists who use conputers have found that they lose control of their prose," Franks says. "One argument is that computers are counterproductive to the creative process because writers become so infatuated with the toy that their intense concentration on their work becomes diluted."

Figures 9, 9*a* and 9*b*. From *This Is Your Life*, by Meg Wolitzer. Wolitzer is the author of the works *Hidden Pictures* and *Sleepwalk-*

*ing*. Much of *This Is Your Life* was written in The Writers Room. Wolitzer bought novelist David Leavitt's computer from him after the typewriter she received for high school graduation fell apart, and has since learned to work comfortably on it. Wolitzer prints out "as soon as I've done anything that I can stand to look at," and revises on hard copy. "I usually work only on the computer," she says, "but if I'm away from it I will do whatever I can to write, which has involved various hotel and motel stationeries."

Figures 10, 10*a* and 10*b*. From *Natalya, God's Messenger*, by Magda Bogin. Bogin is the author of *The Women Troubadours*, numerous translations (including Isabel Allende's *House of the Spirits*) and has worked as a journalist.

The only longhand writing that Bogin does is in her journal. She started her first novel, *Natalya, God's Messenger*, on a typewriter and then moved on to a portable computer. She prints out rarely—every six months—but revises every day on the screen. "The attachment to a series of versions is rooted in typing," Bogin says. "I suspect that we're in a new technology where the gain of being able to work on the screen—and of always having an apparently seamless text—implies the loss of past layers of work. But," she adds, "I can't get too caught up in mourning that."

Figures 11 and 11*a*. From "Cajun Country," a short story by Frances Whyatt. Whyatt, a novelist and poet, is the author of *American Gypsy* and *American Made*. One of the short stories for her current collection in progress has won the PEN Syndicated Fiction award.

Whyatt does all her writing exclusively on a typewriter, penciling in revisions on typed pages and then retyping until the work is finished. "I'm dyslexic, and wrote everything backwards until I was seven years old," Whyatt says, "so writing much in longhand is not an option for me."

Figures 12 and 12*a*.From *Appomatox*, a play-in-progress by Evan Gubernick. Gubernick is a published short story writer and playwright.

Gubernick begins by writing longhand in notebooks "any place but at a desk." After several drafts in longhand, he begins typing and continues to make revisions on typed pages. After producing what feels like a final draft—written in longhand, incorporating all prior revisions—Gubernick lets it "sit for a couple of days. Then I retype for [he hopes] the last time."

Figures 13 and 13a. From *Lamplighter*, a novel by John Simmons. Simmons is the author of *A Teacher's Guide to American Jewish History*, as well as several novels, including *Cried the Piper* and *The Sharing*. He is currently at work on another novel, *Monsieur le Six*.

Simmons sketches plots in longhand, and then moves to his computer, printing out every day, and making revisions on hard copy. "Starting in longhand is important to me," Simmons says. "I feel like emotion and feeling are left out if I don't get to see my work in all its stages."

Figures 14 and 14a. From "Objet d'Amour," a short story by James Boyd Miller. Miller is the author of short stories and a contributing writer to *Millimeter* magazine.

Until recently, Miller would begin his work with longhand sketches, often writing first drafts entirely in longhand. Now he works primarily on a computer, sometimes sketching plots in longhand, revising on the monitor and on printed pages. "The computer has made me much more productive," Miller says. "Writing longhand can put me into a trancelike state where I get lost in the story. With the computer, the lines of communication are more open. I see everything immediately on the screen, as if it's talking back to me as I'm writing."

Figures 15 and 15a. From "Hard Work," by Thomas M. Disch.

MANHATTAN TRANSFERENCE ↗ D̶ARK IN AUGUST

Judith Rossner

[This is the third draft of the first page of the novel eventually named <u>August</u>, part of 100-odd pages that were ultimately, according to the author, "thrown away, or at least consigned to a file someplace."]

Suicide, as Freud was the first to point out, is an act of vengeance and murder, and it is not my intention here to pay homage to the man who intended to d̶e̶s̶t̶r̶o̶y̶ *ruin* my life by ending his own.  Having once been the indirect object of a suicide -- my mother's -- and having come as close to being r̶u̶i̶n̶e̶d̶ *destroyed* as I shall ever come without falling mortally ill, I had developed, long before Vincent mounted his assault on my life, a full arsenal of analytic rhetoric, philosophical positions, songs, jokes and tap dances to deal with matters pertaining to self-termination.  I don't talk to people who talk about it, except in my work, and even there I try to avoid anyone who's more than a casual browser among the possibilities of controling ones own death.  People who consult me to talk about suicide I send to those w̶h̶o̶m̶ *my friend* Bonnie calls the Death Watch Beatles, those serious and eager doctors who are never entirely comfortable until death and disaster enter the room.  People who talk about suicide tend to sound very much the same.  Of course, not all suicides talk.

**Figure 1**

1
~

D R. LULU SHINEFELD opened the door to her waiting room
and said hello to the girl who was scheduled for a consultation. The
girl, whose name was Dawn Henley, nodded coolly.

"Would you like to come into the office?" Dr. Shinefeld asked.

Dawn Henley stood. She was tall, even taller than Dr. Shinefeld,
and quite beautiful, with dark brown, almond-shaped eyes, a star-
tling, almost olive complexion, and honey blond hair cropped to
shoulder length along a straight and severe line. It was July. Dawn
wore white cotton pants, a white T-shirt, and sandals, but she might
have had on a ball gown for the grace with which she preceded the
doctor into the office, sank into the chair facing the doctor's, and
inspected her surroundings.

The waiting room was nondescript, but the furnishings in the office were attractive, if spare. The walls were white; the couch,
brown; the two chairs were covered in a splendid cherry red wool. A
kilim rug with predominating colors of brown, teal blue, and red
covered a portion of the wood floor. Aside from the rug, the artwork
in the room consisted of a semi-abstract painting, in which shapes
suggestive of humans seemed to be posing for what could have been
an old-fashioned family photograph, and a small sculpture resting
on the table at the foot of the couch that was reminiscent of one of
Henry Moore's primordial shapes, an egg embraced by some deli-
cious, unidentifiable object. On the doctor's desk stood a slender
blue vase that held three purple irises. Through an open door near

**Figure 1a**

                    JANE
               (poking him)
          A water bed! When have you ever slept
          on a water bed?

                    KEVIN
          I read that Hugh Heffner has one.
          There supposed to be great for sex.

     She laughs. He kisses her. They kiss harder. He slips his hand on
     her breast. She lets out a little moan, then pulls away.

                    JANE
          ~~You better~~ keep driving. ~~or we're going~~
          ~~to get picked up for loitering.~~

     EXT. CHEVY/OVERLOOK DRIVE - DUSK - ANGLE ON KEVIN AND JANE

                    JANE
          You'll probably meet some snooty girl.

                    KEVIN          *college*
          It's a~~n~~ ~~all~~ men's ~~school~~...

                    JANE
          You'll have parties with those snooty *all*
          girl's ~~colleges~~ *schools*.

                    KEVIN
               (innocent) *we'll be around guys all the time.*
          ~~You're the one going to a co ed school.~~

                    JANE
      *Stet*  Yeah. ~~Maybe I'll meet a future teacher~~ *I'm gonna meet a lot*
          *of exciting guys at the state branch*
                    KEVIN
          *There maybe interesting guys at* Kutztown!
          ~~It's not just teachers at~~
               ~~(moment of silence)~~
          ~~Well, that's it for Overlook Drive.~~

     EXT. END OF OVERLOOK DRIVE - EARLY NIGHT - CHEVY

     pulls off of the road into a wooded area.

                    JANE
          Kevin! *Come on!*

     Headlights off. Car engine off.

     INT. CHEVY - KEVIN AND JANE

     kissing. More heated. She pulls away.

                    JANE
          Not here, Kev. Not for the first

                          2

**Figure 2**

                    JANE
                (poking him)
        A water bed! When have you ever slept
        on a water bed?

                    KEVIN
        I read that Hugh Heffner has one.
        They're supposed to be great for sex.

    SHE laughs. HE kisses her. THEY kiss harder. HE slips his hand on
    her breast. SHE lets out a little MOAN, then pulls away.

                    JANE
        Keep driving!

    EXT. CHEVY/OVERLOOK DRIVE - DUSK - ANGLE ON KEVIN AND JANE

                    JANE
        You'll probably meet some stuck-up girl.

                    KEVIN
        It's a men's college ...

                    JANE
        They'll have mixers with girl's schools.

                    KEVIN
                (innocent)
        You're the one who'll be around guys all
        the time.

                    JANE
        Yeah. Maybe I'll meet a future teacher.

                    KEVIN
        It's not all teachers at Kutztown!

    EXT. END OF OVERLOOK DRIVE - EARLY NIGHT - CHEVY

    pulls off of the road into a wooded area.

                    JANE (O.S.)
        Kevin! Come on!

    Headlights off. Car engine off.

    END TITLES

    INT. CHEVY - KEVIN AND JANE

    kissing. More heated. SHE pulls away.

                    JANE
        Not here, Kev. Not for the first
        time.

                    3

**Figure 2a**

11/30/87
*revisions*

ACT I — β

A turn-of-the-century wood frame house in ~~chronic~~ disrepair.
Renovation has stripped paint ~~from the woodwork~~ and ~~extensively~~ bared lathing ~~through~~ cracked plaster—but no refirbishing has occurred.  Nonetheless, the rooms ~~fulfill~~ their
designated purposes. *(continue to serve)*

LIVING ROOM is furnished with overstuffed couches and chairs
*slip-covers*, ~~with worn slipcovers.~~  There is a stereo system, records, *tapes,*
*outdoors —* posters on the walls, reproductions of familiar art, magazines and newspapers strewn about, ~~and~~ other accumulations of ~~and~~
a ~~bachelor. Door to exterior, and~~ door to adjacent.
*(The room hasn't been cleaned for months.)*

*Door to exterior & leads to adjacent: to adjacent:*

KITCHEN has a serviceable eating table with four chairs,
sink, overloaded dish-drying rack, old appliances, and a
~~wheezing~~ refrigerator covered with notes and reminders.  A
door to exterior. *(flashes)*

BEDROOM has an unmade ~~double bed~~ box-spring-and-mattress on
the floor, ~~bedside~~ lamps and alarm clock also on the floor,
overloaded book cases, a desk buried under papers, a chair, a
bureau with clothes hanging from the drawers and a closet
bursting with gear.  A door ~~leads off-stage~~ to bathroom;
another door to kitchen/living room areas.
*(Tears)*

SCENE 1:  LIVING ROOM, Wednesday evening:

> (BOB WALKER, 40, enters, ~~KITCHEN from~~ outdoors,
> carrying briefcase and sack of groceries.  He is a
> heavy-set, clean-shaven and ~~handsomely~~ *(continually)* disheveled,
> ~~and quite~~ wears an old down parka over khakis, a
> faded workshirt and tie, and a tweed sports jacket.
> He holds the door open)

BOB:      (urgently)  Com'on, com'on in!  I don't want to
          lose the heat.

> *(as. He's)*
> (LARRY KENNEDY, 30, a lean, trim black man with a
> wispy beard, ~~and~~ wearing pressed jeans and a thin
> cotton warm-up jacket over a clean white t-shirt ~~and~~ *He*
> ~~enters~~ carrying a small nylon duffel bag and shakes
> ~~way~~ off the cold) ~~He~~ looks around skeptically as
> ~~BOB leads him into LIVING ROOM)~~

          Make yourself at home.
          *(looking over skeptically)*
LARRY:    You live here?

BOB:      Yeah ~~and now Siobhan too~~.  But there's an extra
          bedroom.  (calling out)  Siobhan!

LARRY:    Siobhan?  What kind of name is that?

**Figure 3**

<u>ACT I</u>

A turn-of-the-century wood frame house in dramatic disrepair.
Renovation efforts have stripped paint and bared lathing
beneath cracked plaster, but no compensating refirbishing has
occurred.  The rooms, meanwhile, are lived in.

LIVING ROOM is furnished with slipcovered, overstuffed chairs
and a couch.  There is a stereo system, records, tapes, out-
dated posters on the walls, cheap reproductions of familiar
art, and magazines and newspapers strew about.  Door to
exterior, and another door to adjacent:

KITCHEN, which has a serviceable table with chairs, sink,
overloaded dish-drying rack, old appliances, and a refrigerator covered with notes and reminders.  A door to exterior.

BEDROOM has an unmade box-spring-and-mattress double bed on
the floor flanked by lamps and an alarm clock also on the
floor, overloaded book cases, a desk buried under papers, a
chair, a bureau with clothes hanging from the drawers and a
closet bursting with gear.  A door to bathroom; another door
leading to KITCHEN/LIVING ROOM areas.

<u>SCENE 1:  LIVING ROOM, Wednesday evening:</u>

               (ZACHARY WALKER, 40, enters carrying briefcase and
               sack of groceries.  He is a heavy-set, clean-shaven
               and comfortably disheveled man who wears a stained
               down parka over khakis, a faded workshirt and tie,
               and a tweed sports jacket.  He holds the door open)

ZACH:     (urgently)  Com'on, com'on!  I don't want to lose
           the heat.

               (LARRY KENNEDY, 30, enters.  He's a wispy-bearded,
               lean black man who wears pressed jeans and a satin
               warm-up jacket over a clean white t-shirt and
               carries a small nylon duffel bag.  He shakes off
               the cold as ZACH closes door behind him)

               Make yourself at home.

LARRY:    (looking around skeptically)  You live here?

ZACH:     (with pride)  Eight years.  (calling out)  Siobhan?
           Siobhan?  (to himself)  I guess she's not home.

LARRY:    What kind of name is that?

ZACH:     Irish.

LARRY:    For a dog?

ZACH:     It's a woman.

**Figure 3***a*

**SIGNE HAMMER**
**WORK IN PROGRESS**

### First draft

Yet he was an extremely sensual man. He loved to eat.
He loved to pick a cigar from his humidor and roll it between his fingers next to his ear to test its freshness,
then pass it under his nostrils for a deep whiff. He would
clip the tapered end, roll it once between his lips to wet
it, light up with a series of short, quick puffs, then lean
back in his arm chair and take a deep, slow drag.

He'd pour his liqueur slowly into its tiny glass and
hold the filled glass up, turning it to take the light, then
lower it and inhale deeply, savoring the sweet fumes. He
rolled the first sip around on his tongue to release its
full flavor, then swallowed slowly, to feel it trickle down
his throat. The fumes and flavors of liqueur, black coffee,
and tobacco mingled and infused his mouth, sent his whole
body into a sweet state of wellbeing. These were gentlemen's
pleasures; they gave away nothing of himself to a women.

**Figure 4**

**SIGNE HAMMER**
**WORK IN PROGRESS**

**Fifth draft**

Not that he wasn't sensual; the men in my mother's life were all sensualists. My father was a man of many appetites, and he liked to convert the little ceremonies of daily life into occasions for their satisfaction. He was master of the rituals that surrounded dinner in those days: fixing the drinks, pouring the wine, carving the roast. Presiding. Smoking his after-dinner cigar. He would pluck it from its humidor and listen to the crinkly music it made when he rolled it between his fingers. (He was tone deaf, but his fingers could feel the sound of good tobacco.)

He drank his liqueur from a small, narrow glass whose thick base was veiled in smoky tones. When he held it up, the liquid amber light shone through the drifting smoke like fire. He held the first sip in his mouth, rolling it slowly over his tongue until it trickled gently down his throat. Mingled fumes of B & B, black coffee, and tobacco infused his mouth, sent his whole body into a sweet state of well-being. These were gentlemen's pleasures; they gave away nothing of himself to a women.

**Figure 4a**

4

the answer to life's pains, perplexities and early morning

unanswerables. I would grab Gordon Ames' manuscript and a blue

pencil from the attache case in the hall, bury myself in the

~~nauseating~~ commercially hopeless midlist (there I go, using that

**word**) jumble of Ames' new and not particularly anticipated novel

and forge out of the tiny smithy of our combined souls a fiction

that, at best, might sell three thousand copies. A fiction that,

with the greatest good fortune, might garner twenty reviews, all

of them ~~out of New York~~ *from the hinterlands (meaning not manhattan)* and ranging in temperature from luke~~warm~~ *cool*

to downright polar.

Gordon Ames' seventh novel was another installment, with

assumed names and so on, in the life, times, temptations and

tr[ia]ls of -- can you guess it? -- Gordon Ames. He figures that

Himself is the most important subject he can put pen to -- one

that will reveal the reader to himself -- and ~~to Himself indeed~~ *ever numerous free*

*(maybe he has often argued that position.)*

~~it seems to be. But as it happens~~ there is no aesthetic choice *of course —*

involved in the matter: the sad and pathetic truth is that the

poor bastard has nothing else to write about. Critics are

forever carping that writers don't write about ~~work~~. But how can *what their characters do for a living*

they ~~?~~ Most writers (Ames is by no means alone, or even the worst *be expected to? in this,*

offender) shy away from ~~close-up considerations~~ *precise descriptions* of where the cash

comes from, and that's because the only job most of them know

anything about -- if you call holing up in a room by yourself and

stringing sentences together a job -- is writing. Fictioneers of

my acquaintance think about themselves constantly and are eager

to rush into print with the latest bulletins on their sexual and

**Figure 5**

the answer to life's pains, perplexities and early morning
unanswerables. I would grab Gordon Ames' manuscript and a blue
pencil from the attache case in the hall, bury myself in the
commercially hopeless midlist (there I go, using that <u>word</u>)
jumble of Ames' new and not particularly anticipated novel
and forge out of the tiny smithy of our combined souls a
fiction that, at best, might sell three thousand copies.
A fiction that, with the greatest good fortune, might garner
twenty reviews, all of them from the hinterlands (meaning
not Manhattan) and ranging in temperature from lukecool to
downright polar.

Gordon Ames' seventh novel was another installment, with
assumed names and so on, in the life, times, temptations and
trials of -- can you guess it? -- Gordon Ames. He figures
that Himself is the most important subject he can put pen
to -- one that will reveal the reader to himself -- and over
numerous free lunches he has often argued that position. Of
course there is no esthetic choice involved in the matter:
the sad and pathetic truth is that the poor bastard has nothing
else to write about. Critics are forever carping that writers
don't write about what their characters do for a living. But
how can they be expected to? Most writers (Ames is by no
means alone in this, or even the worst offender) why away
from precise descriptions of where the cash comes from,
and that's because the only job most of them know anything
about -- if you call holing up in a room by yourself and
stringing sentences together a job -- is writing. Fictioneers

**Figure 5a**

THE DEAL – by Matthew Witten – 1st draft

                          One
                    Scene ~~Two~~ ~~later that day~~

> Lights up, centerstage. A table in a
> restaurant. Bottle of wine and two
> glasses. PETER and JIMMY.

PETER
That's what I'm talking about.

JIMMY
This is what I'm saying.

PETER
That's––

JIMMY
This is what I'm saying.

PETER
Okay.

JIMMY
Where are these guys coming from?

PETER
Okay.

JIMMY
They come in here, think they can do whatever the hell they want.

PETER
No way, hunh?

JIMMY
You got to deal with the people.

PETER
Sure.

JIMMY
The people in the community.

PETER
Of course.  The local people.

JIMMY
The local people.

PETER
Right.

~~2~~ 1

**Figure 6**

*[Handwritten annotations:]*

*Act 2: No restaurant, move the bench downstage.*

*Downstage right: PETER's office. [3rd draft]*
*Upstage right: ALEX's office.*
*Upstage left: JIMMY's office.*
*Downstage left: ALEX's office.*
*Downstage center: restaurant table.*
*Upstage center: park bench.*

**THE DEAL**

Act One

Scene One

*I understand what you're saying.*
*PETER*
*Okay.*

*PETER pours JIMMY wine as lights come up.*

Lights up on JIMMY and PETER, sitting
at a restaurant table centerstage.
On the table, a bottle of wine and
two glasses.

ALEX is in ~~the FBI~~ office, with the
lights down low.

*I mean* JIMMY
The bullshit that's going on...

    PETER
Okay.

    JIMMY
Fucking bullshit!

    PETER
I understand.

    JIMMY
Your company comes in here, ~~and they~~ *and they* think they can do whatever the
hell they want! *..... yet*

    PETER
No way, hunh?

    JIMMY
You got to talk to the people.

    PETER
Sure.

    JIMMY
People in the community.

    PETER
Of course.  Local people.

    JIMMY
Right.

    PETER
Guys like yourself.  Jimmy, this is why I'm here.  The boys with the
bucks heard there was problems in this town.  People who aren't

1

**Figure 6a**

*4th
(and final)
draft*

THE DEAL

Act One

Scene One

Lights up on the restaurant table.
PETER is pouring wine for JIMMY.

Meanwhile ALEX sits in his office,
with the lights down low.

Restaurant noises in background.

PETER
I understand what you're saying.

JIMMY
I mean the bullshit that's going on...

PETER
I understand.

JIMMY
Your company comes in here, and they think they can do whatever the hell
they want.

PETER
No way, huuh?

JIMMY
You got to talk to the people.

PETER
Sure. Guys like yourself.

JIMMY
Right.

PETER
That's why I'm here. To make sure you guys get what you want. (points
to JIMMY's menu) So what would you like?

JIMMY
Expensive place.

PETER
What's your pleasure, Jimmy? The sky's the limit.

JIMMY
I guess I'll have that filet mignon.

PETER

1

**Figure 6*b***

<u>Version I</u>

Here we are in the backyard, the whole family, except my brother. This is the house he rents in Texas. It's flat as far as you can see in every direction, giving wide berth to the sky. That's mostly what you wind up looking at. Garden over there on the left, already half-planted. Even though it's only March, "the year's more fruitful in the south," as Alan, my brother, says. That woman poking at the trees is my mother. Short dyed blonde hair, tallish, robust, black slacks and flowered blouse. She's got that flat-footed step, always feeling her way on the ground. The girl with her is my oldest niece, Allison. Something about her begs to be fat and jolly, the way eyebrows and puffy cheeks crowd her eyes. She hangs up the wash while they chat. Pretty soon she's got to go inside and prepare dinner. Chicken enchiladas, she said.

Haggai is the one wheeling the stroller with the can of mud on the seat. That's a spray bottle of cologne in her hand. She stops and sprays herself with the atomizer. She's five. And the little one who follows her, Deborah, is three. They periodically convene at the mud puddle to pour out mud from the can and then scoop some back up. Mud stains cover their dresses. Over there, playing that paddle ball game imported from east coast beaches, is Saul, the only boy, and with him, my husband, Jeff. Naomi, sitting here at the edge of my chaise lounge, has got the baby on her lap. Naomi has stayed this close to me since about an hour after we arrived.

My sister-in-law, Martha, brings out the sheets for Allison to hang up. Martha's thin, but has that belly that protrudes as if she were permanently five-months pregnant. It's hard to remember her now in the John Lennon cap with inch-long hair barely sticking through, driving fast on the FDR, singing "I Am Woman" at the top of her lungs. She and my brother used to be leftists, back when I was a kid. For my thirteenth birthday, Alan gave me a copy of <u>The Communist Manifesto</u> wrapped with Christmas paper. I tagged along with them to anti-war demonstrations.

**Figure 7**

Version II

"Smell this sweet Texas earth, Ma," my brother says.  "Can you believe
it's only March?" As Alan cups a handful of dirt beneath Sylvia's nose, I can
almost believe he's my same older brother: tall, straggly hair, easy laughter.
His manner, witty but humble, as if he can't help his jokes, still attracts me.
Becoming a Christian hasn't affected his style. Now he leads my mother to the
other side of the garden, out of earshot. Dressed in slacks and a flowered
shirt, Sylvia grasps Alan's arm, her flat-footed step feeling its way between
rows of seeds. To me she seems robust, though she thinks of herself as
overweight.

Alan stops suddenly and faces Sylvia again. His shoulders hunch to ease
the distance between them. Fanlike, his long fingers brush her arm, then wave
toward himself. He seems to be saying you, me, you, me. Sunlight dabs
Sylvia's bleached hair. She laughs and nods, her smile stretching till her back
teeth show.  For the moment she devotes herself absolutely to Alan's words.
They shake their heads in a mirroring of disbelief. Without hearing them, I can
guess that someone did something outrageous, unaccountable, because it has
always been those stories that united us as a family--the ones that led to a
superior amazement.

Beyond Alan's backyard the land running flat in every direction gives
wide berth to the sky. As I sun on a chaise lounge, Alan's five children, all
somewhere near, make me feel lazy and sweet. The baby warms my lap, pulling the
hair on my neck. At my feet, Naomi, with thick braids straining to her waist,
sighs, "Aunt Carol, I wish you had long hair. Then you would look like me."
Naomi has stayed close enough to stroke my hand since yesterday, when I arrived
from New York with Sylvia and my husband, Jeff. He's gone for a walk to the
nearest store, a mile away, to shake off some family dust.

**Figure 7a**

28

Christine fingered a little ~~ivory~~ portrait ⸠of⸡ on ivory

stuck in the back of the drawer
~~Eliza~~ Chiswell, with her snug black silk bodice and a string

her great great grandfathrs
of pearls around her neck. The centerpiece of ~~his takxfv~~

he
fortune was the homestead which ~~sh~~ built amid twenty-five

1868
acres of apple orchards outside of the villa~~ge~~ in ~~1858~~ and

he seemed ~~xxatxfirstx~~ to have built it, ~~as~~ in part, as a kind

of shrine in ~~whe~~ which to ensconse ~~kk~~ his wife. ~~Eliza,~~ according

one
to his diaries, was a pale-skinned prima donna and the ~~only~~

thing in his life that threatened to slip th~~rough his fingers~~

a pear dipped in syrup.
like ~~sivailedxpeanxxxxaxpearxdipped inxhonexxx~~ a honey-dipped

~~xwet~~ sweet sweet
~~pear.~~ She had a ~~xakwakx~~ voice and such unique beauty that the

very sight of her stopped the rocking of men's chairs in front

tucked away
of the post office. Cornelius wanted her out of town, safe

and sound. Luckily, Eliza, who carried herself like a swan

and was fully as voracious
and had that bird's same ~~vaaex~~voraciousness, was more than

content to ~~tinkar~~ tinker and toy in lonliness with the earthly

pleasures her husband could give her. There was, so it is said,
no end to her demand
for them

Figure 8

22

Christine fingered a little portrait on ivory of
Hopestill Chiswell stuck in the back of the drawer with
her snug black silk bodice and a string of pearls around
her neck. Hopestill had been the youngest of five daughters
whose parents still hoped for a boy after she was born and
that was how they had come up with her name. So eccentrically
devoted to her family was she that she wore a wedding gown of
silvery gray to symbolize her sadness at leaving her father's
home.

The centerpiece of her great great grandfather's fortune
was the homestead which he built amid twenty-five acres of
apple orchards outside of the village in 1868 and he seemed
to have built it, in part, as a kind of shrine in which to
ensconce his wife. Hopestill was a pale-skinned prima donna
and the one thing in his life that threatened to slip out
of his hands. She had a sweet voice, like pear syrup, and
such unique beauty that the very sight of her stopped the rocking
of the men's chairs in front of the post office. Cornelius
wanted her tucked away out of town, safe and sound. Luckily,
Hopestill, who carried herself like a swan and had that bird's
same voraciousness, was more than content to tinker and toy in
lonliness with the earthly pleasures her husband could give her.
There was, so it is said, no end to her demand of them.

**Figure 8***a*

**gp**
**genesee**
**PLAZA** / Holiday Inn

All day she had traveled through the dark caves and
tunnels of the World's Fair, and now, finally out in
the wide reaches of ~~daylight~~ sunlight, she could no longer see at all.
That was when her father took the picture: a squinty
girl in culottes standing with her hands out at
her sides enduring the embarrassment. Holiday Inn all around her cameras snapped.
Similar children were posed in front of domes and arches.

All day she had traveled through the dark ~~caves~~ chutes and tunnels of
the World's Fair, and now, finally out in the wide reaches of sunlight,
she could no longer see at all. She couldn't see, and she could barely
hear; either, the same song was still weaving through her: a chorus of singing it
cricket-children singing *It's a small world*, after all, and then in
other languages, each ~~voice~~ version ~~identifiable~~ less recognizable than the last -- until
finally the children seemed to be ~~happy~~ chattering *Gi)ka drytzax faxmazl ab.*
What language Where ~~on the globe~~ was this? she wondered, Slavic, African? She
didn't know, but now it was all over, and she had been shunted
out into daylight. That was when her father took the picture, the
one that proved so important years later. She stood, humiliated in
culottes + thongs, ~~as the~~ ~~adjusted the lens~~ All around
her, other ~~similar~~ children were posed similarly before domes &
arches. ~~Father adjusted lenses. Children sighed heavily,~~
~~flung their arms out, ruining the shot.~~ recognizing
in exasperation, "Hurry up already," she said, ~~having~~ already the
edge to her own voice. There was no love lost between Grace and
that was what he himself had said. Her father was remote
her father; He chronicled everything, he was the family
archivist. Silent, nervous and cold in his short-sleeved
shirts with pens

120 MAIN STREET EAST          ROCHESTER, NEW YORK 14604          PHONE 716/546-6400

**Figure 9**

2.

clipped to pockets, he took pictures of his daughters and, occasionally, his wife. The pictures were always individual portraits, never group shots. ~~They might have all~~ There was nothing to convince anyone that these people ~~comprised~~ made up a family. None of them looked alike, really. Each was imperfect ~~and~~ but in a different way. Only Trace, the ~~little one~~ youngest, was animated, ~~enough to make~~ at ~~age~~ eight, she was all knobbed knees and elbows and nervous jerky motions. She had not slowed down, like her older sisters.

He took a picture of Trace, and it was undistinguished, like the rest of his pictures. Still he placed it in the photo album, sealed it behind plastic.

Years later, when she was ~~forty~~ twenty, and everything had fallen apart, she wanted to look at that time, to preserve it in some ~~sort of~~ amber way, and so she brought back the photo album from home. She took it up to Cambridge on the train, and that night she and Jeff Staples, the boy she was just beginning to love, sat and looked through her childhood.

"I want you to see," she said, opening the big ~~plastic~~ book like a blanket across his lap. First there were the baby shots, and then some backyard barbecues. Finally they were there at the World's Fair in 1963.
Everyone had gone; everyone had distinct memories of it.

**Figure 9a**

186

through a shaft, and showed you the inner workings of the human brain. God, it was great." He paused. "What I remember most," he said, "is how hot it was. I always had to go to the bathroom."

Opal turned the page. There at the top, among the World's Fair series, was a picture she distinctly recalled posing for. She remembered the day well, and how she had traveled for hours through a series of dark chutes and tunnels, and how at the end of the afternoon, finally out in the wide reaches of sunlight, she could no longer see. She couldn't see, and she could barely hear, either. The same song was weaving through her: a chorus of cricket-children singing, "It's a small world, after all," and then singing it in other languages, each version less identifiable than the last, until finally the children seemed to be chattering, "Gluka brznik faxmilgriv." What language was this? she wondered: Russian? Greek? She didn't know, but she couldn't focus on it any longer because her father was making her pose for a picture. She stood, impatient for him to finish, while all around her, other children posed similarly before domes and arches. Fathers adjusted the lenses on their bulky new cameras, and children sighed and swung their arms out, ruining the shot. Opal could not bear the protracted moment between the focus and the click, but her father had a bad temper, so she didn't dare complain. Instead she stood in the invisible frame he had squared off around her, jerking and rolling her eyes.

After the shot her father faithfully rubbed the print with a sponge soaked in some chemical that smelled like toxic salad dressing, and later, after the afternoon was over, he sat in the family room in Jericho, and pressed it into an album, sealing the image of his younger daughter behind plastic.

**Figure 9*b***

Natalya, God's messenger, is my aunt. It was her lucky break right

after the war. ~~Tuesday~~ after V-E day, ~~sixteen~~-~~of~~-~~the~~-~~days~~

~~Friday~~ after paychecks had been handed out, ~~she lost her job as a lathe~~

~~turret operator at the~~ Factory at the conrer of West

4th Street and Sixth Avenue she ~~was~~ got the news: ~~things are going~~

~~to be winding down here, you girls better look for something else. She~~

~~said goodbye to her job as a lathe turret operator at the~~

~~factory and~~ stopped at the newstand in front of Emiolio's pizzeria

There it was: "Natalya, God's messenger, retiring. Established palm-

reading practice for sale. No experience necessary." She ~~jumped on the~~

cross-town bus and Second Avenue. It was an impulse, but what the

hell. She ran up to 8th Street and caught the cross-town bus. Ten minuts

later she was standing at the corner of 7th Street and Second Avenue and

wondering what strange tricks fate had up its sleeve. from where she

could see the ~~sapngly red sign that told her she had come to the Sure~~

enough, the original Natalya, a Ukranian reader advisor, was packing up

her tarot cards and heading south after a lifetime of reading the upturned

palms of weary immigrants and ~~famous~~ actors and ~~singers~~ who came to see

her from uptown. "You'll make a lot of money and meet many interesting

people," she told my aunt, ~~who paid her $100~~, her entire savings, and ~~in those days~~

~~a considerable sum furxim~~, for a sequined turban, a ~~special~~ ruby with

adhesive backing for the middle of her forehead, a crystal ball, ~~four~~

framed pictures of the Bay of Naples, a box of sandalwood incense, a

folding table and a ~~filmxfrimix~~ cards with the names and phone numbers

of all the regular customers.

While Natalya was sweeping up, following her broom around the tiny

store like a cat meticulously licking itself clean, she didn't stop talking.

My Aunt Rita didn't know a life line from a crack in the sidewalk, or the

**Figure 10**

1

Magda Bogin

NATALYA, GOD'S MESSENGER

1.

Natalya, God's Messenger, is my aunt. It was her lucky break right after the war. One Friday afternoon the summer of V-E Day rumors began to fly, and no sooner had paychecks been handed out at the Universal Tool & Die Co. at the corner of West 4th Street and Sixth Avenue, than she and the other girls who worked as turret lathe machinists got the news: the boys are coming home and veterans are going to have priority; you girls better look for something else. It was the end of June and the war in the Pacific was still on, but the first soldiers from the European theater had already been sent home. For women like my aunt, the handwriting was on the wall.

On her way to the subway my aunt stopped to buy a copy of the <u>Daily Mirror</u>. She flipped to the help wanteds, but before she could focus on the listings for machinists her eye stopped short: "Natalya, God's Messenger, retiring. Established palm-reading practice for sale. Two-hundred dollars. No experience necessary." Destiny's own determined arms, as she would later put it, propelled her across town, and ten minutes later she was standing at the corner of East 7th Street and Second Avenue from where, looking east on 7th, she could see the palm-shaped sign halfway down the block.

**Figure 10***a*

2

"I saw your ad," she said when the door to the tiny store was opened by a stooped, beturbaned woman with the bluest eyes my aunt had ever seen; and sure enough the original Natalya, a Ukrainian reader advisor, was packing up her tarot cards and heading south after a lifetime of reading the outstretched palms of weary immigrants and of the rich matrons who came to see her from uptown. "You'll make a lot of money and meet many interesting people," she told my aunt who, after a brief negotiation, wrote out a check in the amount of $140, her entire savings, for a sequined turban, a fake ruby with adhesive backing for the middle of her forehead, a crystal ball, two framed pictures of the Bay of Naples, a fringed red lamp, a folding table with four matching chairs, and a blue damask tablecloth.

"Sit down, darling. I'll tell you everything you need to know."

While Natalya was sweeping up, pressing her broom around the tiny store like a cat meticulously licking itself clean, she distilled her vast chiromantic knowledge into a fifteen-minute course for her successor. My Aunt Rita didn't know a life line from a crack in the sidewalk or the Plains of Mars from the Steppes of Central Asia, but by the time Natalya had finished sweeping, she knew that the left hand was the slate you had been born with and the right what life had written on it. She knew that a thumb could tell you more about a person than a little finger, and that the

**Figure 10***b*

MOTORCYCLE MAN IN A CAJUN CAMPGROUND

He had come in on a motorcycle sometime after midnight and they'd given him the slot next to hers. It had stopped raining, though the ground was soaked and half the slots were under a foot of water, so most the campers, those that weren't in vans or RVs, were still up and talking ~~in those low tones heard in church or when others are sleeping~~.

He was young, nice looking in an intelligent way but not meant to be intellectual. And although the windshield of the big harley was full of bugs and his leather jacket smelled of damp and was cracked and the fake fur collar tacky with sweat and rain and his face streaked with road soot ~~and damp,~~ he had the look of a clean person by nature.

The first thing he did was introduce himself to her, but not in an aggressive way. He just went over and offered to help her with the tent which she'd been re-tieing after an earlier wind had loosened the spokes.

"Been like this long."

"Just since this morning. Yesterday was beautiful."

"Never been in the South before."

"Oh?"

"Yah. Drove straight ~~down~~ from Michigan."

"You're kidding. How far is it ~~to Louisianna~~."

"To where."

"Layfayette."

"Thousand miles."

"That far and you did it straight."

"Well. Stopped for gas and stuff."

"How long it take you."

"Twenty hours."

"Twenty! Don't your legs feel funny."

"Yah. I'm still vibrating, like when you get off a sailboat."

"You sail?"

Figure 11

### CAJUN COUNTRY

He had come in on a motorcycle sometime after midnight and they'd given him the slot next to hers. It had stopped raining, though the ground was soaked and half the slots were under a foot of water, so most the campers—those that weren't in vans or RVs—were still up and talking.

He was young, nice looking in an intelligent way but not meant to be intellectual. And although the windshield of the big Harley was full of bugs, and he wore one of those cracked leather field jackets with the fake fur collars which smelled of damp and sweat, and his face had long streaks of soot running down from it—she saw the care with which he'd stacked and corded in his gear, and had the sense of him as being an otherwise clean and orderly person.

The first thing he did was introduce himself to her, but not aggressively. He just went over, said his name was Ned, and offered to help her with the tent which she'd been re-tieing after an earlier wind had loosened the spokes.

"Been like this long?"

"On and off. Yesterday was beautiful."

"Never been South before. This is my first trip."

"Oh yah?"

"Yah. Drove straight through from Michigan."

"You're kidding. How far is that?"

**Figure 11a**

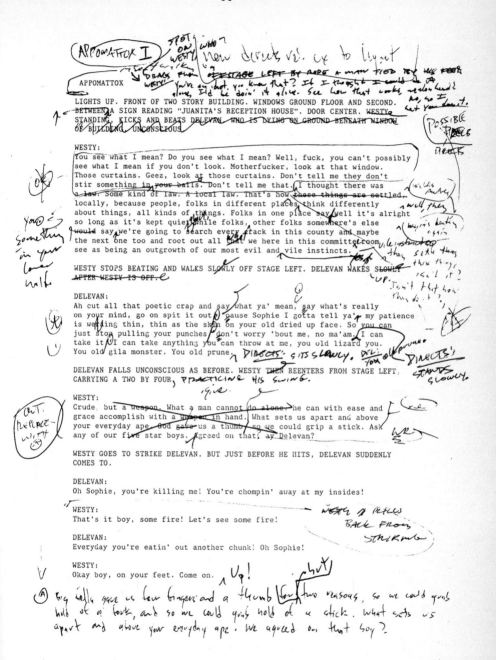

APPOMATTOX I

APPOMATTOX

LIGHTS UP. FRONT OF TWO STORY BUILDING. WINDOWS GROUND FLOOR AND SECOND.
BETWEEN A SIGN READING "JUANITA'S RECEPTION HOUSE". DOOR CENTER. WESTY
STANDING, KICKS AND BEATS DELEVAN WHO IS DYING ON GROUND BENEATH WINDOW
OF BUILDING. UNCONSCIOUS.

WESTY:
You see what I mean? Do you see what I mean? Well, fuck, you can't possibly
see what I mean if you don't look. Motherfucker, look at that window.
Those curtains. Geez, look at those curtains. Don't tell me they don't
stir something in your balls. Don't tell me that. I thought there was
a law. Some kind of law. A local law. That's how these things are settled,
locally, because people, folks in different places think differently
about things, all kinds of things. Folks in one place say well it's alright
so long as it's kept quiet while folks, other folks somewhere's else
would say we're going to search every crack in this county and maybe
the next one too and root out all that we here in this committee room
see as being an outgrowth of our most evil and vile instincts.

WESTY STOPS BEATING AND WALKS SLOWLY OFF STAGE LEFT. DELEVAN WAKES SLOWLY
AFTER WESTY IS OFF.

DELEVAN:
Ah cut all that poetic crap and say what ya' mean, say what's really
on your mind, go on spit it out 'cause Sophie I gotta tell ya' my patience
is wearing thin, thin as the skin on your old dried up face. So you can
just stop pulling your punches don't worry 'bout me, no ma'am. I can
take it I can take anything you can throw at me, you old lizard you.
You old gila monster. You old prune.

DELEVAN FALLS UNCONSCIOUS AS BEFORE. WESTY THEN REENTERS FROM STAGE LEFT,
CARRYING A TWO BY FOUR, PRACTICING HIS SWING.

WESTY:
Crude, but a weapon. What a man cannot do alone, he can with ease and
grace accomplish with a weapon in hand. What sets us apart and above
your everyday ape. God gave us a thumb so we could grip a stick. Ask
any of our five star boys. Agreed on that? ay Delevan?

WESTY GOES TO STRIKE DELEVAN, BUT JUST BEFORE HE HITS, DELEVAN SUDDENLY
COMES TO.

DELEVAN:
Oh Sophie, you're killing me! You're chompin' away at my insides!

WESTY:
That's it boy, some fire! Let's see some fire!

DELEVAN:
Everyday you're eatin' out another chunk! Oh Sophie!

WESTY:
Okay boy, on your feet. Come on.

Figure 12

APPOMATTOX I

SPOT ON WESTY, WHO DRAGS A BODY TIED BY THE FEET FROM OFFSTAGE LEFT.

WESTY:
You're an idiot, you know that? If I thought I could do it alone, I'd
be doin it alone. See how that works melonhead? No, no I bet you don't.
HE STOPS AND UNTIES THE BODY. HE BEATS AND KICKS THE BODY. LIGHTS UP.
FRONT OF TWO STORY BUILDING. WINDOWS GROUND FLOOR AND SECOND. BETWEEN,
A SIGN READING "JUANITA'S RECEPTION HOUSE." DOOR CENTER.

WESTY:
You see what I mean? Do you see what I mean? Well, fuck, you can't possibly
see what I mean if you don't look. Motherfucker, look at that window.
Those curtains. Geez, look at those curtains. Don't tell me they don't
stir somethin in you. Somethin in your lower half. Don't tell me that.
Christ, I thought there was a law. Some kind of law. A local law. That's
how they settle these things, isn't it? Isn't that how they do it? Locally,
right?, because people, folks in different places, well, they think differently
about things, all kinds of things. Folks in one place say well it's alright
so long as it's kept quiet about, while folks, other folks somewhere's
else say we're gonna search every crack in this county and maybe the next
one too and root out all what we here in this committee room see as being
an outgrowth of our most evil and yes vile instincts. Vile instincts.
WESTY STOPS BEATING AND WALKS OFF STAGE LEFT. DELEVAN WAKES UP.

DELEVAN:
Ah cut all that poetic crap and say what ya' mean. Say what's really on
your mind, go on spit it out. Cause Sophie I gotta tell ya', my patience
is wearing thin, thin as the skin on your old dried up face. So you can
just stop pulling your punches. Don't worry 'bout me, no ma'am: (STANDS
SLOWLY) I can take it. I can take anything you can throw at me, you old
lizard you. You old gila monster. You old prune. (SITS SLOWLY) You old
prune.
DELEVAN FALLS UNCONSCIOUS AS BEFORE. WESTY REENTERS FROM STAGE LEFT, CARRYING
A TWO BY FOUR, PRACTICING HIS SWING.

WESTY:
Big fella gave us four fingers and a thumb but for two reasons, so we
could grab hold of a fork, and so we could grab hold of a stick. What
sets us apart and above your everyday ape. We agreed on that boy?
WESTY GOES TO STRIKE DELEVAN, BUT JUST BEFORE HE HITS, DELEVAN SUDDENLY
COMES TO.

DELEVAN:
Oh Sophie, you're killing me! You're chompin away at my insides!
WESTY PULLS BACK FROM STRIKING.

WESTY:
That's it boy, some fire! Let's see some fire!
DELEVAN:
Everyday you're eatin out another chunk! Oh Sophie!
WESTY:
Okay boy, on your feet. Come on. Up!

**Figure 12a**

LAMPLIGHTER                                                          8

Soon she was extradited to Arkansas. She was indicted
for assault with a deadly weapon (pistol whipping) and
*(a shot was fired)*
attempted homicide during the robbery of a Piggly-Wiggly
                                    *actual*
store in Little Rock. ~~The~~ murder charge, which ~~had~~
~~been made in order to involve the FBI, was reduced. But~~
~~Jackie was wanted on other charges as well. She had a~~
~~long criminal record despite her youth.~~

At her trial Jackie pleaded not guilty. She had
            *and*
a poor defense/ no alibi, and ~~was convicted.~~ The state's
attorney labelled her a "vicious, unrepentant criminal
woman" and compared her to Bonnie Parker, John Dillinger,
Kinnie Wagner, and Lizzie Borden. These likenings were
                                          *convicted*
not so much hyperbole as ~~about to~~/premature. Jackie was sentenced
to ten to twenty years in the State Penitentiary.

~~Although~~ Jim Starkwell went to Little Rock that summer
                              *she*      *not*
to try and stand by his bride, ~~no one~~ would let him. ~~He~~
*Although*
He appeared unconcerned about the hatchet, ~~But~~ Jackie
                        *much less talk to him*
would not even see him, / In the newspapers it was
reported that she hated him. Jim Starkwell sat in the
courtroom every day until the trial was over, but Jackie
never even looked at him. "A cruel hoax," observed the
<u>Little Rock Gazette</u>, "does not deserve such loyalty."
After the jury returned with the verdict, Jim went home.

**Figure 13**

LAMPLIGHTER

on the roof and were about to board the elevator, were ruffled and started in a line for the Third Avenue exit. The porter had a time with them. The police took Jackie and threw her into a car and sped away.

Soon Jackie Farrell was extradited to Arkansas. She was indicted for assault with a deadly weapon (pistol-whipping) and attempted homicide (a shot was fired) during the robbery of a Piggly-Wiggly store in Little Rock. There were a half-dozen armed-robbery charges in all. Although the actual murder charge, which had been made in order to involve the FBI, could not be proved, the state tossed everything at Jackie but the kitchen sink. It turned out that Jackie Farrell had an almost lifelong involvement with crime. Her father was the late Bud Farrell, who had robbed the Lilborne National Bank in 1948, capping a long felonious career.

At her trial Jackie pleaded not guilty. She had a poor defense and no alibi. The state's attorney labeled her a "vicious, unrepentant criminal woman" and compared her with Bonnie Parker, John Dillinger, Kinnie Wagner, and Lizzie Borden. These likenings were not so much hyperbole as premature. Jackie was convicted and sentenced to ten to twenty years in the state penitentiary.

Jim Starkwell went to Little Rock that summer to try and stand by his bride. She would not let him. Although he appeared unconcerned about the hatchet, Jackie would not even see him, much less talk to him. In the newspapers it was reported that she hated him. Jim Starkwell sat in the courtroom every day until the trial was over, but Jackie never even once looked his way. "A cruel hoax," observed the *Arkansas Gazette*, "does not deserve such loyalty."

After the jury returned with the verdict, Jim went home.

6

**Figure 13a**

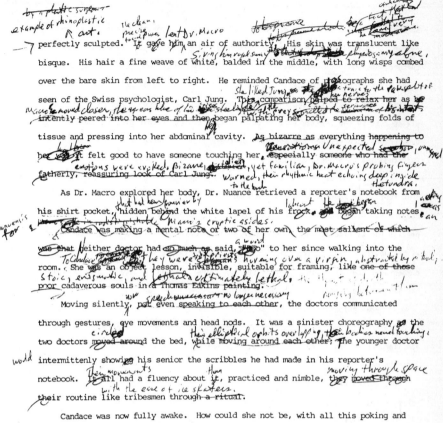

perfectly sculpted. It gave him an air of authority. His skin was translucent like bisque. His hair a fine weave of white, balded in the middle, with long wisps combed over the bare skin from left to right. He reminded Candace of photographs she had seen of the Swiss psychologist, Carl Jung. This comparison helped to relax her as he intently peered into her eyes and then began palpating her body, squeezing folds of tissue and pressing into her abdominal cavity. As bizarre as everything happening to her, it felt good to have someone touching her, especially someone who had the fatherly, reassuring look of Carl Jung.

As Dr. Macro explored her body, Dr. Nuance retrieved a reporter's notebook from his shirt pocket, hidden behind the white lapel of his frock, and began taking notes. Candace was making a mental note or two of her own, the most salient of which was that neither doctor had so much as said, "hello" to her since walking into the room. She was an object lesson, invisible, suitable for framing, like one of those poor cadaverous souls in a Thomas Eakins painting.

Moving silently, not even speaking to each other, the doctors communicated through gestures, eye movements and head nods. It was a sinister choreography as the two doctors moved around the bed, while moving around each other. The younger doctor intermittently showing his senior the scribbles he had made in his reporter's notebook. It all had a fluency about it, practiced and nimble, they moved through their routine like tribesmen through a ritual.

Candace was now fully awake. How could she not be, with all this poking and prodding going on. The young doctor, who Candace thought was kind of cute, had begun kneading her calf muscle and was working his way up to her thigh. Maybe she could convince him to peel her a grape.

All this touching was making her extremely hungry, and between the two appetites competing for her attention, her empty stomach was the stronger of the two. In fact,

**Figure 14**

scratch.  So, much myth and lore to be passed along, doctor to doctor, Macro to
Nuance.  The requisite routines and techniques of planned deprivation, medieval
torture, and wholistic alchemy.  This was an intricate and complex process, and not
to be taken lightly.  The two doctors were all business, speaking in sober,
dispassionate tones, the sub rosa dissonance of medical jargon being exchanged,
giving rise to the feeling that an opinion was forming in thin air, in that
unoccupied space between the movement of their lips.  Candace hated them for their
rectitude and (professional) abstraction.

⟶    Dr. Macro's eyes were a pale blue, almost a grey blue, and watery as if they had
been kept in an aqueous solution too long.  His lips were thin, too, like Nurse
Padgett's.  His nose was narrow, patrician-like, perfectly sculpted.  The clean,
precise facial planes lent Dr. Macro an air of authority.  His skin was translucent
as bisque.  His hair a fine weave of white, balded in the middle, with long wisps
combed over the bare skin from left to right.  He reminded Candace of photographs she
had seen of the Swiss psychologist, Carl Jung.  She liked Jung.

He began palpating her body, squeezing folds of tissue and pressing into her
abdominal cavity.  It felt good to have someone touching her.  Bizarre, alien, yet
familiar, Dr. Macro's probing fingers, were warm to the touch, giving off a heat that
radiated deep inside the tundra.

Dr. Nuance retrieved a reporter's notebook from his shirt pocket, and began
taking notes, jotting down Macro's cryptic asides as he examined her.

Neither doctor had said a word to her since walking into the room.  The two
doctors seemed to Candace like tribal priests hovering over a virgin, abstracted by
ritual, they were stoic, enigmatic, the threat of death hanging between them.

Moving silently, the doctors communicated through gestures, eye movements and
head nods.  It was a sinister choreography as they articulated the space around the
bed in a series of overlapping patterns, moving in and out of one another's way,
precise, never touching; the younger doctor intermittenly showing his senior the
scribbles he had made in the reporter's notebook.  It all had a fluency about it,
practiced and nimble, like ice skaters.

**Figure 14**_a_

"Now here's ~~my plan for Rambo~~ the scenario for the facelift," Sal said, summoning a ~~screen~~ from the ceiling of the room. "Not Rimbaud Chocolates, ~~spelled~~ spelled like that, but <u>Rambo</u> Chocolates, ~~spelled~~ spelled like it sounds, with a slogan that's got some punch, and no more of these ads in French. But a picture is worth a thousand words." He clicked the first slide into place, and the screen burst into giant of fizzy red white and blue letters that promised.

RAMBO!

Straight or gay, he'll blow you away.

~~On~~ Slide 2 followed:
RAMBO!

<u>Attack</u> your problems] with a the man's Chocolate!

Slide 3:
BIFF! POW! ~~SOCKO!~~ BLAM!
RAMBO GIVES A GOOD GOD-DAMN
Slide 4:
RAMBO!
The Chocolate That Led to Victory in Viet Nam!
~~Can~~ lead ~~you~~ to Victory Now.

**Figure 15**

"I think you'll all also agree that the Rimbaud team hasn't been performing up to capacity for a long time. Look at that sales graph! Read the report of the market research team. Three out of four gay consumers in Cheyenne, when asked to name and grade seven male chocolates in order of preference ranked Rimbaud Chocolates last on their list. As to the advertising . . ." Here Sal practised the sneer that his namesake had used to such effect in the unjustly neglected *Dino* (1957, script by Reginald Rose). "Aside from the fact one, that the ads nowhere refer to the product and two, that their scripts are written in a dead language, and three that half the ad budget has been in *The New Yorker* and other scholarly quarterlies that have a combined estimated readership of 4,000, aside from all that they're probably great ads. Not speaking French myself, I wouldn't know."

Burgess-King withdrew a silk handkerchief from his breast pocket and honked into it with discrete defiance.

"It's clear as the nose on the face of the Statue of Liberty that the product needs a face-lift, and here's the scenario I've proposed." Sal summoned a screen from the ceiling of the room and dimmed the lights. "Not Rimbaud Chocolates spelled the French way, but spelled like it sounds – Rambo! And a slogan that promises action, adventure, excitement, aggression – the things that a *man* is looking for in a man's chocolate. Here, I'll show you." He clicked the first slide into place, and the screen burst into giant fizzing red white and blue letters:

RAMBO CHOCOLATES
**Straight or gay, they'll blow you away!**
Slide 2 followed:
**Attack Your Problems
with the Fighting Man's Chocolate**
RAMBO!
Slide 3:
BIFF! POW! SOCKO! BLAM!
RAMBO GIVES A GOOD GOD-DAMN
Slide 4:
RAMBO!
**The Chocolate that Led to Victory in Viet Nam
Can Lead YOU to Meaningful Success!**

"Of course, slogans and promises are just the wax on the paint job. To achieve real success a product has got to penetrate more than a consumer's consciousness. It's got to change his life. When he looks at his face in the bathroom mirror, or better yet in the bedroom mirror, he shouldn't see himself there – he should see the product. 'Mythologize,' as all the marketing textbooks tell us, 'eroticize, and taunt.' Consider the Harley-Davidson motorcycle, one of the greatest products in American history. In its heyday there were seven magazines devoted to the proposition that riding a Harley and wearing its livery were a guarantee of sexual potency and homicidal prowess. For its consumers it provided quite literally a meaning for their lives, as can be seen from its most famous slogan, *Live to Ride, Ride to Live*. Consider, as well, another classic male-oriented product, Jack Daniel's Bourbon. At the turn of the century, many men in the Sun Belt states developed such obsessive product loyalty that they spent from 20% to 50% of their discretionary incomes on not simply the product but on dressing themselves and furnishing their homes with

32

with advertisements for the product. Truly, a marketer's dream come true. The only problem in both these cases was the higher mortality rates associated with frequency of product use. However, Rambo needn't face that dilemma. There is no inherent danger in eating a pound or two of non-nutritive candy. Only if it engendered dangerous levels of aggression among those aspiring to fulfil its image and become, themselves, Rambo chocolate soldiers, only then would there be a risk of the market self-destructing. So let's have a look at the Rambo man."

S al zapped a message to his assistant's auricular splice. "Rod, would you step in now and model that uniform?"

On this cue the doors to the Conference Room parted with a trumpet voluntary, and Rod Steiger, in his new position as Sal's executive secretary, entered in the product livery that would one day earn its own proud niche in the Marketing Hall of Fame in beautiful Tuxedo Park in the state of New York. There Rod stood before the astonished manager, the first recruit to the Legion of the Chocolate Soldiers.

Sal went up to him and plucked a bullet from his bandolier, stripped off the foil, and tossed it to Eddie Albee, the Assistant Marketing Director, who was sitting beside old Walt Whitman. "Eat lead, sweetheart!"

Albee nibbled nervously at the tip of the milk-chocolate bullet, and Rod, blushing with shame but proud to serve General Edibles in any way he could, went round the table dispensing a bullet from his bandolier to each of the managers. As he did so, Sal pointed out, and the managers noted, the other features of Rod's uniform: the I LOVE RAMBO jumpsuit; the chocolate-capped toe of his high-lacing boots (which Burgess-King was encouraged to lick); the Rambo C-Rations backpack with its fifty-pounds of assorted candles that the more gung-ho chocolate soldiers would be able to sell to their buddies in the time-honoured sales-pyramid fashion of Amway and Herbal Life; the Rambo Chocolate Milk canteen prettily embossed with the nude body of the immortal Italian Stallion as movie-goers first got to see him in his earlier porno films, and other chocolate accessories for belt and bandolier too numerous to mention. Sal then ran through the figures R & D had developed concerning possible profit margins on each item of the Rambo uniform.

At the end of the presentation, Burgess-King stood up and, after wiping away the last traces of Rod's toe-caps from his lips with his handkerchief, said: "Sal, I think I speak for all of us here when I say this is a truly interesting and bizarre marketing concept. If consumers can be made to buy one-half the product you're proposing, Rambo could assume a role of leadership throughout the male chocolate industry, and not just in the gay segment. Indeed, it could represent a revolution in the whole field of Recreational Foods. The only problem, as I see it. . ." Here Burgess-King allowed a tinge of sarcasm to colour the polished neutrality of his BBC baritone. ". . how are consumers to be persuaded to cultivate such an intensity of brand loyalty? Short of their being abducted, tortured and brainwashed, which I gather the FDA will not yet allow."

There was a rustling sound round the Conference

**Figure 15***a*

# *INDEX*